Crispus Attucks

Black Leader of Colonial Patriots

Illustrated by Gray Morrow

Crispus Attucks

Black Leader of Colonial Patriots

by Dharathula H. Millender
Illustrated by Gray Morrow

THE BOBBS-MERRILL COMPANY, INC.
INDIANAPOLIS/NEW YORK

PUBLISHED BY THE BOBBS-MERRILL CO., INC.

INDIANAPOLIS/NEW YORK

MANUFACTURED IN THE UNITED STATES OF AMERICA

Library of Congress Cataloging in Publication Data

Millender, Dharathula H.
  Crispus Attucks, Black leader of colonial patriots.

  (Childhood of famous Americans)
  New ed. of: Crispus Attucks, boy of valor. *1965.*
  Summary: Focuses on the youth of the Massachusetts slave who, after joining the colonial patriots in their struggle for freedom, was the first man to die in the American Revolution.
  1. Attucks, Crispus, d. *1770*—Juvenile literature.
  2. Boston Massacre, *1770*—Juvenile literature.
  3. Afro-Americans—Biography—Juvenile literature.

  [1. Attucks, Crispus, d. *1770.* 2. Afro-Americans—Biography.
  3. Boston Massacre, *1770*]   I. Morrow, Gray, ill.   II. Title.
  III. Series.
  E185.97.A86M54   1982   973.3'113 [B]   82-1300
  ISBN 0-672-52735-9   [92]   AACR2

To my parents, Mr. and Mrs. Orestes Hood, Sr.,
and my daughters, Naomi and Justine,
who encouraged me to write this story.

Illustrations

Full pages

Numerous smaller illustrations

Contents

Crispus Attucks

Black Leader of Colonial Patriots

CRISPUS ATTUCKS
SAMUEL MAVERICK
JAMES CALDWELL
SAMUEL GRAY
PATRICK CARR

MARCH 5, 1770.

Visitors Coming

Autumn leaves swirled in the New England air outside the small cottage of Prince and Nancy Attucks. Two little faces were pressed against the windowpane, watching the red, yellow, and brown leaves dance about and drop to the ground. A man and a little boy came strolling across the yard toward the cottage. They kicked at the leaves as they walked.

"Here comes Colonel Buckminster and Tom," said eight-year-old Phebe Attucks to Crispus, who was only four-and-a-half.

"Where?" Cris strained on tiptoe to see.

"I'll bring you a stool to make you taller," said

Phebe, running to the fireplace. She put a stool under the window so that Cris could stand on it and look outside. Then she pointed with the finger of her right hand and turned his head with her left hand to help him see the approaching figures.

"Oh, I see!" said Crispus. He jumped up and down until he lost his balance and fell, striking his head on the window ledge.

Phebe hurried to rescue him, dropped beside him, and started to rub his head. "Are you hurt, Cris?" she asked.

"No," he said, climbing on the stool again and struggling to look through the window. "Let me see." Just as he started to look, he heard a loud knock at the door.

Mrs. Attucks, who was busy cooking at the fireplace, had overheard Phebe say that the Colonel and Tom were coming. When the Colonel knocked, she wiped her hands on a towel and went to the door. Then she flung it open, eager to make the visitors welcome.

"Come in," she said. "How are both of you?" She looked around for Crispus and Phebe, who were standing facing the visitors. "Call your father, Phebe," she said. Then she explained to the Colonel, "He's outside in his garden. He loves it there. It reminds him of home."

The Colonel smiled fondly at her. Meanwhile his son Tom, who was the same age as Cris, sat down with Cris and Phebe near the fireplace. In those days children were supposed to be seen and not heard. All three children sat quietly, hand in hand, pretending not to listen.

WHAT'S CHRIST'NIN'?

Prince came into the house and greeted Colonel Buckminster. Then all three adults sat down to talk before the fire. Soon they started to talk about Cris and said something about christening. Cris overheard them and whispered a question to Tom, but Tom shrugged his shoulders.

"Ask Phebe," said Tom.

"What's christ'nin', Phebe?" asked Cris. The two boys looked closely at Phebe, expecting her to answer. She merely put her finger to her lips and shook her head.

Cris pulled Tom by the hand to a far corner of the room where the beds were located. They could talk there without being rude.

"Are you christened?" Cris whispered.

"I don't know. I never heard of it before," Tom replied. "Let's listen and find out."

Cris nodded his head in approval. The Colonel was saying, "My wife and I thought Crispus should be christened this coming Sunday. What do you both think?"

"Whatever you say, Colonel," said Prince.

"Well, I agree," commented Nancy. "Phebe

14

was christened when she was six months old. We have just put off christening Cris."

"Yes, we've never seemed to set a time for it," Prince added. "Sunday will be a good time."

"Well, I'll speak to Reverend Jonce so he'll be expecting us," said the Colonel. "Then everything will be arranged for Sunday."

Nancy and Prince were slaves in Framingham, Massachusetts, who belonged to Colonel Buckminster. The Colonel was very rich and had numerous Negro slaves and white servants. He owned many acres of land. Many workers were needed to keep everything going.

Prince was the Colonel's favorite slave and had his own cottage, plot of ground, and animals. The Colonel was very nice to the Attucks family. In fact, he was fair but firm with all his slaves and servants.

After Sunday was selected for Cris's christening, the Colonel was ready to go. He stood up and called to Tom to come with him. Then he grasped Tom's pudgy little hand in his own.

Crispus followed Tom. "What's christ'nin'?" he asked.

Smiling, the Colonel put his hand on Crispus's curly head. "It's a way of giving you to the care of God and the church," he said.

"Will Tom be christened, too?" Cris asked, wanting Tom to be with him.

"No, Cris. Tom was christened when he was a few months old. Come, son." The Colonel smiled at the Attucks family again, then led Tom slowly toward the door.

"Bye," Tom called cheerfully as the door closed behind him.

Phebe and Cris hurried to the window to watch the Colonel and Tom walk slowly away through the swirling red, brown, and yellow leaves. Phebe held on to Cris this time to make certain that he wouldn't fall.

16

Presently Cris turned to his father and asked thoughtfully, "Why is my christ'nin' now?"

"We didn't name you until you were almost two years old," his father explained. "You also need to be christened in the church, but somehow we've just kept putting it off."

"Why did the Colonel plan this for me?" Cris wanted to know.

"We belong to the Colonel and do as he tells us," Prince answered. Cris's mother busied herself with her baking.

For a long time Cris said nothing. Then he asked, "What does 'belong' mean, Father?"

"We are members of Colonel Buckminster's household," his father said. "We live on his land and work for him."

Cris looked out the window again and watched the Colonel and Tom disappear through the dusk. "I don't quite understand, but I guess it's all right," he said.

Cris seemed puzzled, but before he could ask another question his mother called to him. "Come to bed," she said. "It's getting dark and I must finish tomorrow's baking."

Obediently Cris prepared for bed, but after he had said his prayers and had been tucked in,

18

he muttered to himself, "I must find out more about this belonging."

On the other side of Colonel Buckminster's house from where the Attucks family lived, there were cabins for slaves. Phebe and Cris couldn't see these cabins from their cottage.

When Colonel Buckminster reached home, he left Tom with Mrs. Buckminster and went to see a favorite slave called Aunt Maria. She was eager to see him because she had been anxious to tell him something for several days. Now she would have a chance to do so.

Aunt Maria was tall with strong, homely features, but her face had a sweetness about it that covered up her homeliness. Her face seemed to show that she was friendly and eager to give happiness to others.

She was well dressed, as were all of the Colonel's slaves. She always wore a snow-white cloth wrapped tightly around her head. Some said that she wore the scarf to hide her head which was almost bald. She had been severely burned as a child, and since then had been careful to keep her head covered.

"What is it, Aunt Maria?" the Colonel said affectionately as he entered the cabin.

She hesitated a moment before saying, "I don't know how to tell you, Colonel, sir." She spoke almost perfect English. She and her husband Cato were pure Africans who had been brought from the West Indies. While there, they had been free to mingle with people and had picked up considerable education.

"Go on, Aunt Maria. Whatever you have to say, you know I will be fair with you. What troubles you so?" The Colonel put his hand gently on her shoulder. Down through the years she had served him faithfully as a nurse for his children and as a house servant.

"Colonel, sir," she began again, without looking into his eyes, "Cato has run away. I knew he was talking about freedom, but I didn't know he would try so soon." She took a piece of cloth from her pocket, wiped away a tear, and shook her head sorrowfully.

"You loved him very much, didn't you, Aunt Maria?" The Colonel showed by this question that he was more concerned about her loss of a husband than about his loss of a slave.

"Yes, sir." She was bewildered. She had been afraid to tell the Colonel for fear Cato would be hunted and mistreated, but the Colonel was taking the news in a kindly manner.

"I won't send after him, if that's what you're afraid of," the Colonel promised. "The men who catch runaway slaves can be very cruel. Cato has served me well, and I don't want him to suffer punishment. I'll miss him, but I can't let his running away upset me. I'll advertise for his return in the Boston *Gazette* tomorrow."

Aunt Maria looked somewhat relieved from her anxiety and grief. She raised her eyes and smiled. "Thank you, Colonel, for your kindness. I would hate to think that poor Cato might be killed. I hope to see him again——" She stopped suddenly without finishing the sentence.

"Do you mean that you plan to join him?" the Colonel inquired in surprise.

"Oh, no, sir," Aunt Maria said quickly. "I am happy here. I will miss Cato, but I can't risk being shot to strike out for Canada." She cupped her hands over her mouth as if she had said something she shouldn't have said.

"Then you know where Cato has gone?" the Colonel inquired.

"I'm not sure, sir," she said without looking up. She was twisting the cloth nervously now and her tears were gone.

"I'm surprised," said the Colonel. "I've always tried to be good to you and Cato. I can't understand Cato's leaving." He walked out, leaving Aunt Maria staring after him.

Inside the big house, the Colonel said to his wife, "Cato has gone. Run away to Canada." There was no expression in his voice.

"Will you send after him?" asked his wife.

"No, dear," the Colonel replied. He dropped wearily into a chair and stared at the logs crackling in the fireplace. His wife sat quietly, giving him an opportunity to think. Finally he spoke again.

"Why did Cato run away?" he asked. "We've been good to him and Aunt Maria. We've taken care of them and given them a good home."

"Has Aunt Maria gone, too?" Mrs. Buckminster asked. "Surely she hasn't gone."

"No, but I can tell that she would like to if she could get a good chance."

Mrs. Buckminster studied her husband's face thoughtfully. Then, softly and haltingly, she said, "Would you like to be a slave? Would you like to have to wait on others, never really having a life of your own? Would you like to feel that you belonged to someone else and weren't free to lead your own life?"

The Colonel rose and started to walk about the room, as if puzzled. "I still don't understand why our slaves shouldn't be happy when we're good to them. We give them good houses and plenty of food to eat."

"But, dear——"

The Colonel abruptly changed the subject and started to hang his coat on a peg. "Let's talk about something else, something more pleasant. I've arranged with Prince and Nancy to have Cris christened at church next Sunday. They agree with all our plans."

"Prince and Nancy are happy here, aren't they?" asked Mrs. Buckminster.

"I don't know, but they seem so," said the

Colonel. "They are my favorites here. I hope they are happy."

"I know. Would you like something to eat before we retire?" she added.

"No, thank you, my dear," he answered. "I am a bit tired tonight."

And so the Colonel's day ended.

Where Are Your Parents?

PRINCE got up early to tend his garden. Cris awakened and watched his father move quietly about the cabin. He and Phebe slept in a trundle bed, which was pulled out from under the big bed at night. They slept on a fluffy feather mattress with their heads buried in goose feather pillows.

For a few moments Cris merely watched. Then he slipped out of bed, dressed, and tiptoed over to join his father.

"Good morning, Father," he whispered.

"Good morning, son," Prince said, putting logs on the fire. "You're up early this morning."

"Yes, Father. I didn't sleep much last night. I was thinking and wondering."

Prince filled a large earthenware cup with steaming coffee. "May I have some coffee, Father?" asked Cris.

"No, but I'll warm you some milk." For several minutes father and son sat quietly together. Only the soft sound of the crackling logs could be heard.

Finally Prince broke the silence by saying, "What's on your mind, son?"

Cris, who had been sipping the warm milk, set down his cup, as if ready to start a serious conversation. "Will I always belong to Colonel Buckminster, Father?"

"I'm afraid so, son. Why do you ask?"

"I'm not sure. I never knew about it before— this belonging business, I mean." He looked down at his feet and wiggled his toes in his shoes. It was obvious that he was puzzled.

Prince looked hesitatingly at the little boy sitting by the flickering shadows of the fire. Then he said, "Many years ago I was a little boy just like you. I was happy and carefree, and all that I had to do was to run and play. No one told me what to do except my father, who was the king of our country."

Prince paused and sipped his coffee. Cris looked at him intently.

"My father had seven sons, and each of us learned to do the thing he loved best," Prince went on. "I loved to grow things in the soil, so I learned as much about farming as I could. A few years later, my father put me in charge of a large group of tribesmen."

Cris looked at his father quickly, as if surprised. "You mean they belonged to you?"

"Yes, son, but we didn't exactly look upon them that way. They helped us grow rice, and millet, and vegetables."

"Vegetables in Africa, Father?" Cris's eyes grew wide with wonder.

"Yes, son. We grew yams, groundnuts, pumpkins, melons, and beans."

"Why did you leave, Father?"

"I didn't want to leave, son, but we had a war. My father was killed. We all were taken away as slaves."

"Then you belonged to someone, Father?"

"Yes, I suppose you might call it that, but that was the way life was then. If there was a war and you were captured, you had to accept whatever happened." Prince sat with the cup at his lips, slowly sipping his coffee, and stared into the fire.

"Please tell me about Africa." Cris pulled up a stool close beside his father's chair. He waited for his father to speak.

Prince smiled and his eyes lighted up. He was happy to change the subject. "Our home was

beautiful," he said. "There were trees, grass, and flowers everywhere. The weather was warm all the time, never cold as it is here."

"You mean you never saw snow?"

"Not until I came here. We had rain in Africa, but we never had snow."

"It would be nice to have more warm weather here, but I would greatly miss the snow. Tell me about your father."

"Well, my father was known best for his efforts to make the people of his kingdom prosperous. He encouraged them to be farmers and to trade with other people."

"What does 'prosperous' mean, Father?"

"It means successful," Prince replied. "My father told his people that they needed to go to school in order to learn how to be prosperous or successful. Our schools were different from the schools in this country, but they were suited to the needs of our people. They taught our people

31

how to read and write our own language. We had doctors and scientists, too, and many other kinds of workers."

"It's good for people to know how to read and write," said Cris.

"That's right. Do you want to hear more?"

"Yes, Father, please." Cris moved his stool closer to his father's chair.

"My father's empire was divided into large sections. Each section was governed by a man known as a Fari, and each Fari directed a number of chiefs known as Nois. These men were in charge of the large cities.

"My father also had a large army. We needed an army because our enemies were always trying to seize our possessions." Prince paused to stir the fire and put another log in the fireplace. Then he sat down again and went on.

"We had banks and courts, too, and markets where many kinds of things were sold. Traders

32

came to these markets from Europe and Asia. They came to purchase beautiful objects made of gold, silver, and ivory, and other objects made of wood, stone, or clay."

"Did traders come from America?" asked Cris.

"Not so far as I know, though people from America may have come to visit our country. We had visitors from many parts of the world, and some people came to attend our schools."

Prince paused again to stare thoughtfully at the fire, then went on almost as if speaking to himself, "Then my father was killed and I was sold as a slave."

"How awful, Father!"

"No, not awful, son. Anyone captured during a war was thought of as a slave. That's the way things were in those days. Slaves were the property of the chief of a tribe or the head of a family, and could be kept or sold as the owner wished. Most of them became trusted members of the tribe or family and were free to carry on many activities. But others were sold and taken to other countries. I was one of these."

"What happened to you?"

"I was sold to some traders from the West Indies, who brought me here."

"You mean Colonel Buckminster was a trader?" Cris's eyes opened wide.

"No, son. He bought me from the traders."

"Was I born then?"

"No, that was several years ago."

"Well, if I wasn't born then, how can I belong to the Colonel now?" Cris asked.

Prince looked thoughtful and chose his words carefully. "Because I belong to the Colonel and you are my son. We live in this house which belongs to the Colonel, and we live and work on the Colonel's land. Now you can see what it means to belong. We are fortunate to belong to the Colonel rather than to someone else."

Cris was not ready to end the conversation. "I'm not sure I like it, Father," he said without getting up. "I'm not sure."

"You've always been happy, son, and there's no need to change now." Prince poured himself another cup of coffee from the pot that hung over the fire. Cris held out his little cup for more milk, and the two sat down to talk a while longer.

"Father, are we talking man to man?" Cris asked presently.

Prince smiled broadly. "Yes, son."

Cris drew himself up tall, then sat back and sipped his warm milk. "Not many slaves have their own cottages," Prince explained. "I have my own plot of ground just as I might have had in Africa, though not as large. You have always been happy here, and you can keep on being happy. The important thing is that you are my son and I'm proud of you. You will have many growing pains, as you are having now."

Cris smiled at his father's words. "Growing pains, did you say? You mean that I'm growing up? Well, I guess I am." By this time the milk in the cup was gone. Cris put down his empty cup, ready to end the conversation and to go outside with his father.

"Come on, son," said Prince. "Let's go work for a while in the garden."

A Day at the Big House

"It's time to get up, Rachel," Phebe said to her doll. "We must get ready to go to work at the Big House."

Rachel, the doll, was made out of a corn cob. Her face was painted on white linen cloth that covered one end of the cob. She was dressed almost exactly like Phebe and her mother. She wore a green dress and had a small white kerchief about her neck and a tiny brown bonnet on her head. Phebe took Rachel everywhere, even to the Big House where the Colonel and his family lived. She pretended Rachel was alive.

"Mother, do you think Cris would mind if I

let Rachel hold some of his marbles in her lap?" Phebe asked. "She likes the marbles."

Mrs. Attucks paused to look around. She was pushing the children's trundle bed under the high bed in one corner of the room. "No, Phebe, don't touch Cris's marbles. He doesn't want you to play with them."

"I won't harm them, Mother," said Phebe. "I just want to put them in Rachel's lap."

"Forget the marbles and get ready to eat breakfast," said her mother. "We must hurry over to the Big House and start our work." She moved toward the fireplace.

Phebe laid her doll on the foot of the bed. She placed her down gently and spread a cover over her, as if she were a real living baby. "I'm sorry that I can't find anything for you to play with this morning," she said. "I'll be back after breakfast." She followed her mother across the room to the fireplace.

While Phebe and her mother got breakfast at the fireplace, Cris and Prince worked outside, milking the cows and feeding the hogs. Prince fed the Colonel's animals, and Cris took care of the two cows and six pigs that belonged to the Attucks family. Prince carried on many extra duties because the Colonel was a member of the General Court or legislature and had to be away from home much of the time.

"Let's hurry with the porridge, Phebe," Mrs. Attucks said. "The menfolk will come in hungry in a little while."

"Why do you call Cris a 'menfolk,' Mother?" Phebe asked. "He's just a boy."

"Yes, but he's as big as most boys who are eight or nine years old, and he works as hard. He even talks and thinks like an older boy. Now hurry and set the table."

Phebe was a good worker and liked to help her

mother carry on household duties. She set the table for four persons, giving each person a porringer, a wooden spoon, and a mug.

In a few moments Cris came in and rushed to the fireplace to warm his hands. He held both hands before the fire.

"Is it cold outside?" Phebe asked.

"No, but it's chilly," he said. "What are we having for breakfast? I'm hungry."

"We're having the same old thing, porridge," Phebe said, without looking up.

Presently Prince came in and sat at the head of the long, narrow table.

"Come to the table, children," Mrs. Attucks said. When everyone was seated, she bowed her head and quoted from the Bible, "Give thanks unto the Lord, for He is good."

Then Prince prayed, "All help comes from above. Come, Jehovah, be Thou our guest at meat."

The moment he was finished, Cris seized his spoon and dug into the porridge hungrily. "Ouch!" It was hot and burned his tongue.

"Not so fast, Cris," Phebe said. "You eat like a hungry pig."

"Take your time," said Mrs. Attucks. "It's not good to eat so fast. You must learn to eat more slowly."

At first Cris frowned, but almost immediately he looked up and smiled. "Well, I'm hungry, but I'll eat more slowly."

Prince asked for more coffee, and sipped it slowly and silently. He seemed to be thinking and planning the day's work. When everyone was finished eating, he said, "Let us pray."

All the members of the family folded their hands and bowed their heads.

Prince started to pray. "We give thanks unto the Lord, O most high. He has given us health and peace, food, clothing, and shelter. Delight thyself also in the Lord, and He shall give thee the desires of thy heart. Amen."

"Amen," said the others.

Soon Prince and Cris left the cottage to finish their chores. Mrs. Attucks and Phebe went to the Big House to help Mrs. Buckminster.

"Good morning, Nancy, and how are you, Phebe?" said Mrs. Buckminster. Phebe curtsied. "I see you brought Rachel." Phebe smiled and hugged the doll tightly.

"How do you always know what to do in the Big House?" Phebe asked her mother.

"I have a job for each day," explained Mrs. Attucks. "On Monday I wash. On Tuesday I iron. On Wednesday I bake. On Thursday and Friday I give the house a thorough cleaning, and on Saturday I get ready for Sunday."

"You work hard here and you work hard at home, too," said Phebe, puzzled.

"Yes, but here in the Big House I have many

persons to help me," explained Mrs. Attucks. "I'm in charge of the workers."

"What does that mean?" asked Phebe.

"It means that I tell other persons what to do and see that the work is done. Now get busy and do your work here."

Phebe put Rachel in a corner by the hearth and reached for a large turkey wing with the feathers still attached. With this feathered wing she carefully brushed the hearth in front of the

fireplace. Then she helped some of the other girls sweep and dust.

The girls did not talk as they worked. Mrs. Attucks objected to their talking because Prince didn't want Phebe and Cris to be close friends with other slaves. The others were not happy, he said, and he wanted his children to be happy.

When the cleaning and dusting were finished, the other girls left, but Phebe stayed with her mother. She sat on a stool in the corner of the kitchen, holding Rachel, and watched her mother begin the baking. For some time, she was quiet and thoughtful.

Presently she looked up and said, "Mother, what is the difference between servants and slaves? There are some of both here, but they seem to do the same kinds of work."

"That is a hard question to answer," said Mrs. Attucks. "Let's see. How can I explain? All the servants are white and come from parts of the world where other white people live. The slaves, including your father, were brought here from Africa. They were called Negroes here." She paused to think of the right words. She wanted to make things clear to the little girl.

"Are you a Negro?" Phebe asked.

"No, I am an Indian, but I have accepted the position of your father, who is a slave."

"What does that mean—'accepted the position'?" Phebe asked.

Mrs. Attucks sighed. "Dear, I really don't have time to answer questions this morning. I must get on with the baking."

"Just this one, Mother, and I won't ask any more," Phebe promised.

"Well, Indians and Negroes are friendly, and many Indian girls marry slaves. When an Indian girl marries a slave, she must live where he lives and follow the same laws that he obeys. Now do you understand?"

When Mrs. Attucks saw the serious, thoughtful expression on Phebe's face, she went on. "There are two kinds of workers here on the Colonel's plantation, servants who are white and slaves who are Negro. None of us is free to come and go as he wishes, but the servants have more freedom than the slaves."

She tied a fresh white apron around her waist, rolled up her sleeves, and put a fresh white cap on her head. She scrubbed her hands with a brush, using strong, soapy water. Then, with quick skillful movements, she measured and sifted flour, and rolled and cut cookies, tarts, and pies. When all these things were ready to bake, she put them in long baking pans and shoved them in a hot oven at one end of the fireplace.

"Are slaves un-free forever?" Phebe asked after the baking started.

"Yes, they are," explained Mrs. Attucks, "but they can be just as happy as other people. I chose this kind of life to be with your father, and I am happy. You can be happy, too. Servants become free," she went on. "They serve their masters for a period of years in order to pay for having been brought to this country. When their time is up, they become free like other white people."

Phebe asked no more questions. Mrs. Attucks was glad, because she was eager to go ahead with her work. "I must hurry with my baking or I'll never finish it," she said.

A NEW SUIT FOR CRIS

When the baking was almost finished, Mrs. Buckminster came into the kitchen. "My, how good it smells here, Nancy."

"Thank you," said Mrs. Attucks, smiling.

"Is Cris ready for tomorrow?"

"Yes, Ma'am, he is."

Mrs. Buckminster held up a white suit. "Here is a new suit for him to wear. I made the suit for him myself."

Mrs. Attucks' face beamed, showing deep gratitude. "Oh, thank you, Ma'am."

"You're quite welcome, Nancy. It isn't every day that a child is christened."

When Mrs. Attucks and Phebe returned to the cabin, Prince and Cris were already there. A big fire was roaring in the fireplace, and the table was set for dinner.

Mrs. Attucks smiled at Cris. "Did you set the table, Cris?" she asked.

He smiled with pleasure, but before he could speak Phebe said, "That's girl's work."

"Don't tease Cris," said Mrs. Attucks. "Tell him that you are sorry for what you said about his setting the table."

Phebe hung her head. "I'm sorry, Cris. I didn't mean to hurt you." Then, in an attempt

48

to make him feel better, she blurted, "You have a new suit for the christening."

"Phebe!" cried Mrs. Attucks, who had expected to tell Cris about the suit later.

Cris dropped his head. "I don't want a new suit, and I don't want to go to church." He started toward the bed in the corner.

"Cris." Prince followed him. "Remember what I told you today?"

"Yes, I remember," Cris said without looking up. "We're children of praying Indians and I have to go to church and be christened."

There was no feeling in his voice. Phebe thought he was going to cry. She felt terrible about having said things to upset him. "What are praying Indians?" she asked.

Mrs. Attucks did not answer at once. Then she said, in a far-away voice, "When I was a little girl, I belonged to a tribe of Indians known as the Natick Indians. They were Christian Indians who had been taught about God and the Bible by a man named John Eliot. This Christian leader lived long before I was born, but my parents still followed his teaching."

"Where are the Indians now?" Phebe asked.

Mrs. Attucks paused again and Prince went to her and put his arm around her shoulders. Then she said quietly, "Someday I'll tell you about King Philip's War and what happened to my people, but let's eat supper now."

The supper was eaten in silence. Afterward Prince heated some water over the fire and got out his razor and soap. As he shaved, he paused now and then to talk with the children. Then he read a chapter from the Bible and said a prayer.

Mrs. Attucks bathed the children and told them to wait until she warmed the bed. She put hot embers in a brass warming pan and moved the pan back and forth between the sheets of the trundle bed. She kept moving the pan until she thought the bed was warm. Then she pulled out the pan and said, "All right now, get in bed!"

Phebe and Cris hated to leave the warmth of the fireplace, but their father whispered, "Good night!" and gave each a little shove. They hurried across the room, jumped into the bed, and pulled up the blankets.

"Good night," their mother whispered.

The cottage grew quiet. In a few minutes the children were fast asleep.

Cris Is Baptized

WHEN SUNDAY morning came, Mrs. Attucks had a hard job. She tried to get the children to dress quickly for church.

"I'm ready, Mother," Phebe reported.

"You look very nice," said her mother. "Sit on the stool and don't move." She patted Phebe's snow white bonnet and smiled.

"Come, Rachel." Phebe took her doll and went to sit beside her father. He was watching Cris, who had a rebellious look on his face.

"I don't like this suit, and I don't want to go to church," Cris was saying as his mother helped him to dress. She pretended not to hear.

"Now you're ready," she said at last with a proud smile. "You look just right, son."

"I don't want to go," Cris said again.

"We must do many things we don't like, Crispus," said his mother firmly. She smoothed her dress and picked up her Bible.

"Come, children," Prince said. He went outdoors and the others followed him.

The church bell was ringing, when the members of the Attucks family reached the church. All the slaves sat in the gallery, and the white people sat in the big room below.

"I see Tom down there," Cris whispered to his mother on the way to a seat. "Why can't I sit down there with him?"

"You have to sit here because this is our part of the church," answered his mother. "The part down there is for Mr. Buckminster and other white people. Climb into your seat and be quiet. The service will soon begin."

At last Cris settled down between his father and mother. A janitor closed the church doors and everyone was quiet. The minister climbed the five steps to his pulpit in one end of the building. Before him stood a small hourglass filled with sand. When he began his sermon, he turned the glass up and preached until the last grain of sand had run through.

In front of the pulpit sat the elders with stern faces, facing the congregation. In front of the elders sat the deacons, also with stern faces. The chief elder arose and stood stiffly. Then he looked up into the gallery and spoke loudly to the congregation.

"Today we will have the baptism of Crispus Attucks. He comes through arrangements made by Deacon Buckminster. Will the parents bring the child down from the gallery?"

Proudly Prince and his wife arose and motioned for Cris to come with them. Cris hesi-

tated, obeyed silently, and followed them down to the main floor of the church.

When Prince and his wife and Cris reached the main floor, the elder continued. "Will Colonel and Mrs. Buckminster come forward?"

The Colonel and his wife arose and came to the front of the church. Then the elder said, "This child has been taught to keep the Sabbath and to observe civil order. He is a descendant of the praying Indians."

The elder stepped back and the minister moved forward to face the little group. Cris looked at Colonel and Mrs. Buckminster and noticed that they were smiling. He looked at his parents and noticed that they also were smiling. There, standing downstairs in front of the congregation, he felt important and began to smile, too. Somehow he liked the ceremony.

The minister sprinkled water on Cris's head and spoke the necessary words. He put his hands gently on Cris's head and prayed. Then Cris and his parents made their way back to the gallery. A murmur of approval went through the white members of the church. The slaves were silent, but showed that they approved, too.

On the way home Cris was very quiet. When he reached the house, he went to the bed and took off his white suit. "You know, I really felt important today at church," he said. "I made a fuss about something that was really nice. I enjoyed being baptized, Father."

"I'm glad you did," said Prince.

Sunday was a quiet day in the Attucks house. It was a quiet day in every home on the Colonel's big farm and in the whole town of Framingham. After long hours at church, people went home to eat, read the Bible, sing hymns, and pray. The people did no work, except things that were absolutely necessary. Women set tables and brought out food to eat, but let the soiled dishes go until Monday. Men took care of the animals and milked the cows, but did nothing else.

Cris enjoyed the Sunday of his baptism more than he enjoyed most Sundays. Several times his parents had to remind him that this was Sunday and that he was not to laugh or play. He felt like doing both.

"Being baptized is a serious matter, son," Prince said as they were milking the cows.

"I know, Father, but I feel good all over. I guess I feel grown up."

Prince smiled. "Yes, everyone was proud of you. Your mother was proud, Phebe was proud. Everybody in the church was proud."

"And I was proud," said Cris. "Sometime I want Mother to tell me about the praying Indians. Do you think she could tonight?"

"She might. It's time you should know."

"Well, I'll ask her," said Cris.

Who Were the Praying Indians?

PHEBE WAS just finishing setting the table for Sunday dinner when the menfolk came in. Her mother was at the fireplace putting pork and vegetables in a large serving dish.

Cris tiptoed over to his mother. "My, everything smells good!" he said. "Will we have hasty pudding, too?"

"Yes," answered his mother, as she carried the dish to the table.

Cris smacked his lips. On Sunday he wasn't supposed to act like this, but his mother was glad to see him in a good mood.

The family ate in silence until Mrs. Attucks

brought the hasty pudding to the table. Then Cris had to say something. "Here comes the pudding. I just can't wait to get some."

"Maybe you can't, but don't talk so loudly," said his mother. "Remember, this is Sunday."

Phebe ate her hasty pudding silently. Both she and Cris hoped that their mother would tell them about the praying Indians. Finally she looked at her mother and said, "After supper will you tell us about the praying Indians?"

"Yes," said Mrs. Attucks. "This Sunday when Cris was christened will be a good day to talk about them."

Prince read several verses from the Bible and the family sang a hymn and recited the Lord's Prayer. Mrs. Attucks and Phebe cleared the table and stacked the dishes. Prince put fresh logs on the fire and stirred it up. Then everyone sat in front of the fireplace.

"Many years ago, when this land was first

settled by white men," Mrs. Attucks began, "there was a minister named John Eliot. This minister, called Apostle Eliot, loved the Indians and wanted to teach them about God.

"In 1650, he persuaded some Indians to found a religious settlement in Natick township, not far from here. He got the government to give the land to the Indians in exchange for other land in the western part of the colony. The Indians who settled in Natick became known as the Natick Indians.

"Natick meant 'the place of hills.' The land around the settlement was fertile and the Indians prospered. They planted corn and raised cattle, horses, and hogs.

"There were only eleven families at first, but others came until there were seven separate villages, only a few miles apart. Each family was given a hornbook with the Lord's Prayer on it in their Indian language and in English.

Each family also was given a sampler with words of faith on it."

Mrs. Attucks brought out a carefully wrapped package and opened it. "Here are the hornbook and sampler that were given to my great-grandfather," she explained. "My grandmother gave them to me when I was ten years old."

LORD'S PRAYER ON MRS. ATTUCKS' HORNBOOK

OUR FATHER	HEAVEN IN,	HALLOWED
Nushun	Kesukqut,	Quttianatamunach

THY NAME,	COME	THY KINGDOM,
ktowesuonk,	Peyaumuutch	kukketassutamoonk,

THY WILL		DONE EARTH ON
kuttenantamoonk	nen	nach ohkeit

AS	HEAVEN IN,	OUR FOOD
neane	kesukqut,	nummeetsuongash

DAILY	GIVE US	THIS THIS DAY,
asekesukokish	asamaiinean	yeuyeu kesukod,

AND	FORGIVE US	OUR SINS
kah	ahquontamaunnean	nummatch-essongish

AS	WICKED-DOERS		WE FORGIVE	THEM,
neane	matchenekuk quengig		nutahquontamounnonog,	

ALSO	LEAD	US		NOT	TEMPTATION IN,
ahque	sagkom-pagunaïinnean		en	qutchhuaonqanit,	

OH	DELIVER	US	EVIL
wehe	pohquohwussinnean		wutch match

FROM,	FOR	THINE	KINGDOM
itut,	Newutche	kutahtaun	ketassutamoonk

AND	POWER		AND	GLORY
kah	menuhkesuonk		kah	sohsumoonk

FOREVER	AMEN.
micheme	Amen.

WORDS ON MRS. ATTUCKS' SAMPLER

CHECKESOM	JEHOVAH	KEKOWHOGKOW
Wash	Lord	My soule

AMANAOMEN	JEHOVAH	JAHASSENMETAGH
Take away	Lord	My stony heart

The children looked at the objects with interest. "How old are they, Mother?" asked Phebe.

"I was told they were made in 1659," her mother replied. "Someday when you are older,

I will teach you how to read and speak the Indian words." She put the hornbook and sampler on the table and went on with her story.

"Apostle Eliot taught the Natick Indians to read and write, to carry on different kinds of work, and to live in clean homes. He helped them to set up rules or laws to govern themselves. He helped them to establish a court with an Indian Justice of the Peace. This court served all seven towns, but each town had a sachem or chief to govern it.

"The village in which my great-grandfather, John Uktuck, lived was governed by a chief, named Wuttusacomponum, who was called Captain Tom. He was a wise man who set a good example for his people. My great-grandfather helped Captain Tom to keep the village in order."

"What became of Captain Tom?" Phebe asked.

"That is really part of another story," said Mrs. Attucks, "and a sad story, too. For a while the Natick Indians were prosperous and happy. Then a bloody war broke out between certain other Indians and the whites. The war was started by Indians that were not Christian, but the Natick Indians were drawn into it.

"The war started after the death of the great sachem Massassoit, who had ruled the Indians in this part of the colony. Massassoit had been very friendly with the first white settlers here, and never had any trouble with white people throughout his life. After he died, his two sons became sachems—first Alexander, who soon died, and then Philip. The whites did not trust Philip and ordered him to appear before the General Court and to give up his firearms. Philip knew from this action that the whites no longer trusted his people.

"Philip and his people were unhappy. They

saw their land being sold to white men piece by piece until they themselves were crowded into two small areas. Philip thought these sales of land were unfair.

"Besides this, Philip and his people liked their own religion and refused to learn about God and the Bible. They were brought into court many times to explain their actions and purposes. This made them angry. They had always been independent and did not like to be looked down upon or governed by others, especially by white men. They wanted to be left alone."

"Did Philip's people ask the praying Indians for help when the war started?" Cris asked.

"No, they didn't," Mrs. Attucks said. "However, not all the praying Indians were as honest and faithful as they should have been. It was really a praying Indian who started the war. He wasn't a member of our tribe, however."

"Tell us about him, Mother," Phebe said, moving her chair closer to her mother's.

"Well, in January, 1675, a Christian Indian named John Wussausamon, who had worked for Philip, told the English that Philip was plotting against them. Philip's people became angry and killed the man as a traitor. Then the white people arrested the murderers and hanged them.

"When this happened, Philip and his people began to worry the whites in all sorts of ways, sometimes even destroying property. Philip's medicine men warned that a war might end badly, but Philip did not listen to them. Finally a white man shot an Indian. Shortly afterward a war broke out. Before it was over, it brought an end to the praying Indians."

Mrs. Attucks paused for a moment, and during the silence Prince got up to put another log on the fire. Phebe and Cris then turned to their mother. "Is that the whole story?"

"No," she replied, "but there is only a little more. Philip thought the praying Indians would side with the English and didn't trust them. The English were afraid of all Indians and didn't trust the praying Indians either. The poor praying Indians suffered from both sides in the war. Finally some of their villages were broken up and destroyed.

"Our tribe was allowed to continue as a community for a short period, but things were no longer the same. At last Captain Tom and his family, my great-grandfather and his family, and a few others were taken prisoners.

"All of them were taken to Boston, put on trial, and convicted. The women and children were spared, but Captain Tom and my great-grandfather were hanged. They held to their Christian religion and died praying to God. After the war, the praying Indians were separated and mixed with other tribes."

Mrs. Attucks stopped. She seemed relieved to have finished her story. Putting her hands in her lap, palms down, she studied them silently. The dimly lighted cottage was silent except for the crackling of logs in the fireplace.

At last Cris said, "What happened to Philip in the war?"

"I thought you would ask that," she said. "Philip fought on, but many of his people were killed, and he was hunted from one hiding place to another, like a wild animal. At last his wife and son were captured, and his son was sold into slavery. Then Philip gave up."

"How sad!" Phebe said, tightly hugging her doll. "May I look at the things on the table again, Mother?"

"It is too late, Phebe, but you may look at them again in the morning," said her mother. "Now it's time to go to bed."

Phebe and Cris rose obediently and went to

the bed in the corner. Their mother prepared the bed for them with the warming pan.

"I liked the story you told us, Mother," Cris said. "I am proud to be your son."

Mrs. Attucks smiled as she took the warming pan out from between the covers. "I'm glad," she said. "Good night now."

She put the warming pan in its place by the fireplace. Then she and Prince smiled fondly and proudly at each other.

Trouble at the Attucks Cottage

THREE YEARS had passed since Cris was baptized, and now the Attucks household had three children. "Little Brother," as the family called him, was a year old. Both Phebe and Cris were very happy about him.

For several days now Little Brother had been crying and whining. This evening he seemed to have taken a change for the worse. His face was flushed, and he was much more restless than he had been before. Phebe sat on the bed beside him, bathing his face in cool water. Mrs. Attucks stopped to look at him, great alarm showing on her face. She felt afraid.

72

"Watch him closely, Phebe, while I try to get help," she said, throwing a heavy shawl over her shoulders. "I'll go to see whether I can get Aunt Maria to come. She will have medicine and will know what to do. Your father and Cris are still at the Big House doing their chores. They may be back before I return."

"Yes, Mama," Phebe said. She knew that her mother was frightened, and she was frightened, too. She watched Little Brother carefully. Every breath that he took seemed to hurt him.

Mrs. Attucks hurried along the path around the Colonel's house to the back where the slaves' cabins were located. Soon she came to Aunt Maria's cottage, which was near the Big House. She noticed that the door was ajar and she heard a voice inside, but hesitated when she heard one of the slaves talking to Aunt Maria.

"If you have not heard from Cato," he was saying, "why would you try to join him? Canada is a wild country, and it's a long way off. What do we know about it? And besides, Cato might be dead when you get there."

"That's what I say, too, Maria," said the slave's wife, who had come to the cabin with her husband. "Colonel Buckminster is very good to us here. Cato should not have left. I certainly would not go to Canada looking for him."

Aunt Maria started to talk and Mrs. Attucks overheard her mention Cris. "Yesterday Cris was here," she said. "He told me about talking with a sailor who had come out from Boston. His ship had just come from Canada, and he said that he had seen Cato up there."

Mrs. Attucks stepped inside, but in the shadow of the door, no one noticed her. Several slaves, both men and women, sat facing the fire, which provided the only light. Aunt Maria stood at one side of the fireplace, facing them.

An old man, leaning on a home-made cane,

spoke up. "Cris is only a boy and may have been mistaken. Also there are many Negroes named Cato and the man the sailor mentioned may not have been your husband."

"How can you reach Canada?" said another slave. "You'll have to go to Canada by ship, and you can't get on a ship without a permit. If I were you, Maria, I would forget about following Cato and try to be content."

Maria dropped her head in thought. The group began to sing softly. In the middle of their song, Aunt Maria looked up and saw Mrs. Attucks standing in the doorway.

"Come join us, Nancy," she called. Then, seeing the expression on Mrs. Attucks' face, she rushed to her side and cried, "What is the trouble? Why do you look so worried?"

The singing stopped and everyone turned to look at Mrs. Attucks. "My baby's sick," she explained. "Little Brother is very sick. He's red hot and in great pain. Help us, Aunt Maria, please come to our cottage to help us."

"The fever!" the group cried in unison.

"Yes, perhaps he has the fever," Aunt Maria said. "I'll come with you. First let me get some roots and herbs to take along."

Aunt Maria went to the fireplace, gathered up several small bags, and put them in the pockets of her dress. Then taking Mrs. Attucks by the arm, she led her gently but firmly toward the door and out of the cabin.

When they reached the Attucks cottage, Prince and Cris were already home. Prince was leaning over the baby's bed, helping Phebe to take care of the baby. He looked worried.

"Help us, Aunt Maria, please," he begged.

Aunt Maria went to work at once. She told Phebe to continue bathing the baby's face and asked Cris to bring a mug of hot water. Then she took some green leaves from one of the bags in her pockets and dropped them into the water. She stirred the mixture briskly for a moment with her fingers. Finally she put a few drops on the baby's lips and watched him, but she didn't look pleased.

She took a dark pill from another bag and softened it with water. Then she squeezed liquid from the soft pill on the baby's chest and watched him again.

Cris and Phebe sat side by side near the fireplace and watched Aunt Maria in silence. They could see that their father and mother were frightened, and for this reason they were frightened themselves. They didn't really understand what was happening.

For a while the cottage was silent except for the crackling of the fire and the baby's restless, labored breathing.

After a time Aunt Maria rose and went to the bed again. She repeated the treatment, bending

over the baby and gently rubbing its chest. As she worked, she looked more and more worried. At last she looked up and shook her head. "I'm sorry," she said. "He's gone. It was too late. Lord have mercy!" She bowed her head.

For the first time Cris and Phebe saw their mother cry. She cried furiously.

"There, dear," said Prince. He patted her shoulder in an effort to console her. Suddenly Aunt Maria began to sing and Cris joined her.

> "Steal away. Steal away. Steal away to
>   Jesus.
> Steal away. Steal away home. I ain't got
>   long to stay here.
> My Lord, He calls me. He calls me way up
>   yonder . . .
> The trumpet sounds within-a my soul.
> I ain't got long to stay here."

Aunt Maria left after the song ended. "Where did you learn that song, Cris?" Phebe asked.

"From Aunt Maria," Cris said.

"You know her?" Phebe was surprised.

"Yes, I like to go behind the Big House," he said. "We have fun there."

"Will you take me sometime?"

Before Cris could answer, his mother said sternly, "I don't want either of you to go behind the Big House! Your father has told you many times, Cris, not to go there."

"Don't make me promise, Mother," Cris said, "but I'll try."

CRIS AND PHEBE TAKE THE FEVER

Late that night the Attucks family needed to call Aunt Maria again. Phebe and Cris became feverish and had severe pains in their chests. As Cris drew each breath, he felt as if a sword were running through his chest. Phebe felt almost as bad, but didn't have such high fever.

When Aunt Maria arrived, she started to work promptly. Once more she dug into the pockets of her dress and pulled out some green leaves and dark-colored pills.

"We must work fast," she said. She put the green leaves in hot water and told the children to drink some of the mixture. She asked them to put the pills into their mouths to soften them. Then she took the moistened pills in her brown hands and squeezed liquid onto the children's chests. Afterward she rubbed their chests to work the liquid in.

"I'm going to leave you some pills," Aunt Maria said to Mrs. Attucks. "Keep putting the liquid on the children's chests until the pain goes away!"

Mrs. Attucks took the pills. "Thank you," she said gratefully.

"Keep the children warm and don't fall asleep," cautioned Aunt Maria. "Come for me again, if they aren't better by dawn. Now I must rush back home, for many people have the fever."

"Do you think the children will be all right?" Mrs. Attucks asked with terror in her eyes.

Aunt Maria patted her shoulder. "Pray and take care of them. We slaves are strong."

"But my baby went so fast."

"He was young," Aunt Maria said. "These children are big and strong. Look at Cris. He's not quite seven, but he's as big as a boy of eleven. He's a fine boy."

Prince came forward. "You know Cris well, don't you?" he said.

"Yes, he visits us often."

"When he comes, do you teach him to rebel against his master?"

Aunt Maria turned in the doorway and looked Prince squarely in the eyes. "I don't teach him to rebel against anybody or anything," she said, "but he has strong feelings. He has a mind of his own, and I can't teach him anything he doesn't want to learn."

"Don't encourage him, Aunt Maria. He's just a boy. Let him be content."

Aunt Maria turned to go, but said, "Don't try to be different from us. Don't keep Cris from his people. It is not right. Good night."

Prince and his wife continued watching all night, and by morning the children could breathe without pain. Both parents fell asleep, fully clothed, on the foot of the bed. They were relieved. Phebe and Cris were cured.

Why Is My Name?

As SPRING BEGAN to awaken the grass, trees, and flowers, the Attucks family worked more and more outdoors. One morning Prince said that this would be a good day to make soap. Mrs. Attucks had been saving scraps of fat all winter to put into the soap. "Take the scraps outside to your father," she told Cris.

Prince got a large barrel, removed one end, and bored holes in the other end. He set the barrel upright with the holes on the bottom. Then he filled the barrel with ashes, which he had saved from the fireplace.

Finally he said to Cris, "Bring me a pail of

water." Then he poured the water in the open end of the barrel. Soon a dark liquid started to trickle out the bottom.

"Look, Father, something black is coming out the bottom of the barrel!" Cris cried with alarm. "Something black!"

"The water passing through the ashes makes lye," explained Prince. "We need the lye to boil with the scraps of fat or soap grease." He brought a big pan to catch the dark liquid.

"How can these things make soap?" Cris asked, watching his father mix the lye and grease in a large kettle.

"Watch and you'll see," said Prince. He built a fire under the kettle and asked Cris to bring stools for them to sit on. Then they sat and waited for the liquid to begin to boil. Neither of them said anything. Cris wriggled his toes and stared at the fire.

When the pot began to boil, Prince got up and

stirred the mixture with a stick. Cris got up, too, and stood close by, watching his father intently. He stayed close by the kettle even after his father sat down again. Presently Prince said, "Don't get too close, son."

Cris moved back, although he did not seem to be listening. Suddenly he said, "Father, why is my name Crispus?"

Prince frowned. "Why do you ask?"

"Well, most people have names like Tom, Jim, Henry, or John, but no one around here has a name like mine." Cris was eight now, but he still couldn't forget what had puzzled him at four-and-a-half.

"Yes, your name is different from other names," Prince said as he rose to stir the soap again. "It has a special meaning."

"That's what upsets me, Father. I don't like being different. May I change my name to Tom, or maybe John?" Cris was serious.

"No, son," Prince said firmly. "You have a good Indian name. Your mother and I want you to take after your Indian ancestors."

"But I'm not an Indian. I'm a slave. You said so yourself," Cris protested.

"That is true, but slaves are a mixture of many bloods," said Prince. "You are pure African and Natick Indian. Since we live in your mother's country, and not my native Africa, I want you to be like your Indian ancestors."

Cris was silent. His mouth was set in a firm, straight line.

"Indian names always mean something, such as courage, honesty, or beauty," Prince went on to explain. "Your mother's family was important, so we use her last name."

"But why do I have a funny name like Crispus? Nobody else has that name."

Prince stirred the liquid and gently led Cris back from the kettle. "Crispus is a Christian name," he said. "It means beauty."

"Beauty? I'm not beautiful."

"Let me finish, son. When you were born, your hair was curly, so you were named for St. Crispin, a Christian leader who lived long ago.

Mrs. Buckminster told us about the Christian leader and his name. Your mother wanted you to be a Christian and important."

"Does Crispus mean important?"

"No, but Attucks does. Attucks means 'small deer,' and deer are the most important animals to Indians. The Indian word is 'Ahtuk.'"

Cris seemed to be deep in thought. Finally he smiled. "Well, I guess it's not so bad to be different, Father. I will try to be important. I'll do something important someday."

Prince looked pleased. "Just lead a good life, son, and be happy."

Phebe came from the house. "Mother and I have been making candles," she said. She carried a candle in her hand. She felt light and gay, but could see that Cris was in deep thought.

She looked at him and stopped smiling. "What's wrong, Cris?"

"Nothing," he said, starting for the house.

"I'll go inside to see whether Mother needs any help with the candles."

"We have finished making candles," she called after him, but by the time she spoke, he was almost to the door. With a puzzled look on her face, she followed him to the house to see what, if anything, was wrong.

Prince went on stirring the soap, wearing a smile on his face.

Fun Behind the Big House

COLONEL BUCKMINSTER had one of the largest farms around Framingham. He needed many slaves and servants to help run the farm and to take care of his other affairs. He was an important man in the community.

His house was the largest building on the farm. It was a two-story frame building, painted white and surrounded by a lawn as smooth as a green carpet. Here and there on the lawn were trees and bushes, and at the front and sides of the house, there were borders of flowers. In summer a large tree shaded the porch at the front of the house.

There were other buildings back of the Colonel's house—barns, stables, sheds, and cabins for the slaves and servants. The cabins were small, but each had a garden and a shed and pen for a cow and a few pigs.

The servants were white persons, known as indentured servants. They had agreed to work for the Colonel for a certain number of years because he had paid their way to Massachusetts. At the end of their agreement, they would be free and could do as they wished.

The slaves, on the other hand, were mostly Negroes. They belonged to the Colonel for life and never would be free. Either the Colonel had bought them or, like Cris and Phebe, they were children of his slaves.

The Colonel owed much of his success and happiness to his slaves and indentured servants. For this reason he treated them kindly and tried to help them live well. Prince and his wife and many others liked the Colonel and appreciated his kindness. They believed they should be contented and not worry about the future. There were others, however, who were unhappy and wanted to be free. For some reason, young as he was, Cris was interested in this group.

One morning when Cris was ten years old, he and his father sat in front of the cottage, resting and talking. The sun was shining, there was a fresh breeze, and the odor of growing plants filled the air.

Prince had a few things that he wanted to say to Cris. "You were behind the Big House last night," he said.

"Yes, Father, I was there, but I didn't stay," said Cris.

"What goes on back of the Big House that makes you want to go there?" asked Prince, eagerly awaiting his son's response.

"The people there have fun, Father," said Cris.

"They laugh and sing and dance and tell stories. They have popcorn, too."

"Why are you excited about popcorn?" Prince exclaimed. "We've had popcorn here at home ever since you were able to remember. After all, the Indians had popcorn first."

"I know, Father, but you don't understand."

"You're a big boy now, Cris," Prince said seriously. "You're ten years old and it's time for you to settle down. You must choose the kind of work that you want to do here, and then learn to do the work well. Most boys of your age already know what they want to do. You must stop this nonsense."

Cris said nothing for a while. He wiggled his toes as he often did when he was troubled. Finally he said, "Father, I won't always be here. Someday I'm going to be free and when I'm free, I'll work on a boat."

Prince sighed. "You're old enough to think for

94

yourself and not let others talk you into things. Our life isn't bad, is it?"

"No," Cris admitted.

"We hardly know that we're slaves here," Prince went on. "We have our own cottage, our own piece of land, and our own animals. We have plenty of food to eat and good clothing to wear. We can keep on living this way as long as we wish. Why should we want anything else?"

Cris hung his head. At last, he looked up and said, "The trouble is that we're even different from the other slaves, Father. Who wants to be different?"

"Is that what the slaves behind the Big House tell you, son? Is that how they convince you that something is wrong with your life? Is that the reason you want to be free?"

Cris nodded.

"Look around you, son," Prince went on. "The Colonel gives me responsibility to run the farm here, and he rewards me by allowing me to live better. People with responsibility always live better than others. That's the way it was in Africa and that's the way it is here. I can't understand why you should worry about being different as long as you have an opportunity to live well. Sometimes in this life it's good to be different."

He paused to watch Cris, but there was no expression on Cris's face. Then he added, "Don't let others make you unhappy, son. You're young and have your whole life before you."

Suddenly Cris lifted his head. "Slaves can be punished," he said. "They can even be whipped if they don't obey orders."

"All people can be punished if they don't do right," said Mrs. Attucks, just returning from the Big House. "God takes care of people who believe in Him and people who do right. If we do right, we don't need to worry about being punished. Our master, Colonel Buckminster, is very kind to us. He's not the kind to punish people, and no one else will bother us."

"I'm just mixed up," said Cris, "but somehow I seem to want to be free rather than a slave. I know that here with Colonel Buckminster we live almost as if we were free."

"I must get back to work," said his mother, "but let me remind you of one important thing. You must think for yourself and not let others influence you. Some of the other slaves may not be happy, but it won't help to stir up trouble. You can't afford to be mixed up with them. Just do what is right, and you'll be happy."

GAMES AND SONGS

For a time Cris tried to obey his parents and stay away from the cabins behind the Big House. Before long, however, he began to slip away and to spend more and more time there. He liked to mingle with the slaves.

The slaves' cabins were smaller than the Attucks cottage, and not so well furnished. Each cabin had a fireplace for heating and cooking and a small collection of pots and pans. Each contained a bed, a table, and a few chairs and stools, and each was neat and clean. Each yard was covered with grass, shrubbery, and flowers. Behind each cabin there was a garden and a shed and pen for animals.

The slaves who worked in the Colonel's house lived in somewhat better cabins than the slaves who worked on the farm. The difference in the cabins often caused hard feelings among some of the slaves.

Strangely enough, even though Prince ran the farm and his wife ran the Big House, no one seemed to envy them. Prince always tried to treat the slaves squarely and they believed in him. He frequently made trips through the slaves' quarters just to talk with them. He was never too busy to spend time with them, even though he wanted Cris to stay away from them.

One morning when Cris was twelve years old, he asked Phebe to accompany him to the cabins. They went behind the kitchen of the Big House with its huge fireplace, where their mother was baking bread, biscuits, and cookies. They stopped at the smithy to watch Jonah, the smith, repair a broken wheel. Jonah liked his work and was contented with his food, shelter, and clothing. He refused to join other slaves in complaining and talking about freedom. Like Prince and his wife, he was happy to belong to the Colonel. He believed deeply in God and liked to pray.

"I like Jonah," Phebe said as she and Cris moved on from the blacksmith shop to the row of cabins where the slaves lived.

"I like him, too," Cris said, "but I don't under-

stand him. I don't understand Father and Mother, either. They don't seem to care because they belong to somebody."

"Cris!" Phebe was shocked.

"Well, they don't, but I can't help but care." Cris walked along kicking the dirt of the path with one shoe. "I don't like the idea of belonging to someone, not even to the Colonel. Father said I should think for myself, and I've been thinking. I just don't like the idea of being a slave all my life."

Next Cris and Phebe passed the stable and the coach house. They stopped to talk with the coachman, who was cleaning the Colonel's fine coach.

In a little while the two children returned home, but that evening, after supper, Cris went back to the cabins. Now that he was twelve years old, he was allowed more freedom than he had when he was younger. He liked to talk with different slaves and learn about the day's happenings. Most of all, however, he liked to take part in the storytelling, dancing, singing, and playing games.

This evening he joined a group of slaves who were visiting Aunt Maria. "Cris," she said, "why don't you lead us in 'Did You Feed My Cow?'"

"Yes! Good!" everyone cried.

Cris rose and stepped into the center of the circle. He looked at the faces around him. "Did you feed my cow?" he called.

"Yes, sir!" the others answered.

"Will you tell me how?" he asked.

"Yes, sir," they chorused gleefully.

"What did you give her?"

"Corn and hay." They began to sway rhythmically. "We just gave her corn and hay!" They began to clap their hands.

Aunt Maria suddenly stepped into the circle beside Cris to lead the Juba dance. She stamped her foot and patted her hands twice, and the others followed suit. The dance was continued for several minutes.

When the dance stopped, Cris called excitedly, "Did you milk her good?"

"Yes, sir," the others answered.

"Did you do it like you should?"

"Yes, sir."

"How did you milk her?"

"Swish, swish, swish." They moved their hands as if they were milking a cow. "We just milked her swish, swish, swish."

Now Aunt Maria began her Juba dance again —stamp, pat-pat; stamp, pat-pat; stamp, pat-pat; stamp, pat-pat. The rhythm grew stronger and louder as the group picked it up, stamp, pat-pat; stamp, pat-pat; stamp, pat-pat.

Suddenly a weird whistling sound outside the cabin interrupted the dance. Aunt Maria stopped leading the dance and all the noise and clapping died down. "What was that weird whistle?" the people asked one another.

"That was my father," said Cris. "He wants me to come home. Good night." He disappeared quickly into the darkness.

Prince was waiting for Cris outside the cabin. "What was all that noise?" he asked.

"We were playing 'Did You Feed My Cow?' but we hadn't finished. I had two more rhymes to call out when you whistled."

"Your mother was worried about your staying so late," Prince said as they walked toward the cottage. "She wanted me to come after you."

"She shouldn't worry," said Cris. "I'm twelve years old and five feet and five inches tall."

"Yes, you're twelve years old, but you're still our son. We worry about you when you stay away from home in the evenings."

"I'm sorry, Father," said Cris. "The next time I go behind the Big House, I'll tell you. I just have to go there. The older I become, the more I want to go there."

"Then you won't stop going there?" Prince looked a little surprised.

"No, Father, I can't," said Cris. "Those are my people. I belong there."

Prince looked sad. "Be careful then, Cris. Don't let them get you into trouble."

"I'll be careful, Father."

Cris Must Pick a Trade

ALL BOYS on Colonel Buckminster's farm were taught trades or special kinds of work in order to be prepared for adult life. One day when Cris was thirteen years of age and nearly six feet tall, the Colonel sent for him. He wanted to talk with Cris about a trade.

"What would you like to learn to do, Cris?" he asked. "You can learn to be a blacksmith, a miller, a cooper, a cabinetmaker, a shoemaker, or a farmer."

"I would like to work on a boat, sir," Cris said without hesitation.

"But I have no boats, Cris."

"I know sir, but that is the kind of work I would like to do. I've spent a lot of time down by the river, watching boatbuilders put planks and timbers together to make boats. I've watched men put masts and sails on boats to make them go. From time to time I've had opportunities to talk with sailors who work on big ships on the ocean. They have come out here from Boston while waiting for their ships to be loaded and unloaded. I want to work on a large ship."

"Unfortunately there is no way I can help you," said the Colonel, calmly studying the tall boy before him. Through the years he had watched Cris grow and had come to think of him as a member of his own family. He had come to realize that Cris was independent and felt that he was watching and waiting for something.

"Since I have no boats, Cris," the Colonel added with a broad smile, "suppose you learn to drive the carriage until you find something else that you would like to do."

Cris realized that there was nothing more the Colonel could say or do, so he said obediently, "Thank you, sir. I will do my work well and try my best to please you." He smiled and waited for further instructions.

"Go tell James to teach you how to drive," the Colonel went on. "Let me know each day how you are getting along."

"Yes, sir," Cris said and hurried away. He had always liked Colonel Buckminster and respected him. He had hoped that somehow, even though the Colonel had no boats, he would let him become a sailor. Now, it was clear that he never could become a sailor as long as he was a slave. All he could do was to hope that something would happen later. So for the present, he must try to be content.

When he got home that evening his mother

was preparing supper. "Did you decide what you wanted to do, son?" she asked.

"Yes, Mother," he said. "I'm supposed to learn to drive the carriage."

"How good!" exclaimed Mrs. Attucks. "You can drive for the Colonel!"

"No, I don't want to drive the carriage," said Cris. "I want to become a sailor on a big ship and travel on the sea. I have talked with sailors who have come out here from Boston. They have told me many interesting things about their work and the things they have seen. Someday I mean to become a sailor and learn about the sea myself." Cris spoke and looked as if he meant what he said.

"You can't become a sailor as long as you're a slave," said his mother, "unless your master has ships on the sea. The Colonel has no ships. Why don't you get that sailor idea out of your head and be contented to learn something here?"

She stopped working and looked at him seriously. Then she added, "You used to like to watch Jonah in his blacksmith shop making showers of red sparks and hammering on his anvil. You could become a smith and learn to make things for the Colonel, just as Jonah does."

"I know, Mother," said Cris, without raising his head.

Nancy went on. "You used to watch the cooper making barrels and talked about how skillfully he worked to fit the wooden staves together." She paused expectantly but Cris only let her go on talking. "You used to stop at the cabinet-maker's shop to get curly shavings of wood to bring home to Phebe. Many times you said that you wanted to learn how to make beautiful tables, beds, and chairs. Do you remember?"

"Yes, I remember, but I was only thinking how nice it would be to make them for you."

Nancy smiled and patted his head. He was

sitting in front of the fire, deep in thought yet trying to listen to what his mother said. Soon she gave up talking and hurried to set the table for supper.

After the supper dishes were washed and put away, the family drew chairs together in front of the fire. Phebe and her mother brought out some of their sewing. Cris wriggled his toes and studied them thoughtfully. Prince thought of things that he needed to do tomorrow for Colonel Buckminster.

At last Prince said, "What type of work did you choose, son?"

"I didn't choose any, Father. I told the Colonel I wanted to work on a ship, but he asked me to learn to drive the carriage."

"That was the best he could do, son, because he owns no ships."

"I know, Father," said Cris, "but if I were free I could work on a ship."

Mrs. Attucks looked at Cris, disturbed. Then she looked at Prince, hoping he would speak.

Prince spoke sternly, "You're growing up, Cris, and need to use your head. Try to be content here with the Colonel. You can't change things."

"I know, Father, but I can try."

"Cris!" exclaimed his mother. "You don't know what you're saying. You don't need to try to change things. Time will do that."

"Your mother is right, Cris," said Prince. "Stay

away from the other slaves and try to be happy. Learn to drive the carriage and learn to drive it well. Learn to do anything well that the Colonel tells you to do. Remember, he is getting old and tired, and I wouldn't want him to sell you and break up our family."

Cris looked shocked. "Would he do that?"

Prince shrugged his shoulders. "He could, son, but I hope that he won't. I would be surprised if he sold you without talking with me first. But try not to annoy him."

"I'll try, Father," Cris said firmly. And he meant just that.

Cris Is Sold

CRIS TRIED HARD, but he just couldn't be content driving the carriage. Every now and then, he wandered away to do other things.

One evening when the Colonel needed him to drive the carriage, he couldn't be found. Prince went from cabin to cabin to locate him, but no one had seen him.

When Cris returned home, Prince said, "Where have you been? The Colonel wanted you to drive, but we couldn't find you."

"I was down by the river," said Cris. "Why didn't he get Tom to drive the carriage? We both drive about the same, Father."

114

"You're supposed to be here when the Colonel wants you," Prince said flatly.

"I know," said Cris. "I'm just property for the Colonel to order about." There was a certain bitterness in his voice. "If I didn't have to drive the carriage, I would really enjoy it. What is wrong with me anyhow? Why am I like this?" Now he seemed to be upset with himself.

"I don't know, son," Prince said. "Maybe it's because you don't stop to think about things. Maybe it's because you're trying to grow up too fast. Just stop to think, son."

The next day important things took place at the Attucks cottage. Prince and Nancy were outside, in the yard, when Colonel Buckminster came to see them. He looked bent, worn, and very tired. His speech was slow.

"I'm sorry," he said hesitatingly, "but I must sell Cris. He isn't happy here, and I'm too old to watch over him any more. Recently I talked with Deacon Brown about him. The Deacon has boats and has promised to let him work on a boat. Will you tell Cris to be ready to leave in the morning?"

"Then you've already sold him?" asked Mrs. Attucks, startled.

"Yes, Nancy."

She started to cry, softly at first, then deeply as if her heart was broken. Prince put his arm around her.

"I'm sorry, Nancy," the Colonel said sadly. He looked at her as if surprised that she should feel so upset. Then he turned to Prince. "I'm sure you understand, Prince. Cris isn't happy here. I've tried to be kind to him, but I can't manage him any more." The Colonel seemed to be pleading with Prince to approve of his action.

Prince nodded as if to agree, but in his heart he had lost all respect for the Colonel. The thing that he feared most had happened, but he had never thought that it would actually happen. Cris had been sold without his being consulted. He just couldn't believe it! The Attucks family was being broken up by the Colonel, the man he had trusted so much and the man he had loved so well.

"Deacon Brown will be good to him and give him an opportunity to work on a boat," said the Colonel. He was trying to explain his actions.

"I understand," said Mrs. Attucks without looking up. Most of all she wanted the Colonel to go and leave her alone with Prince. She was certain that Prince, too, wanted the Colonel to leave, but he was speechless.

The Colonel felt deeply sorry for Prince and his wife. He had never seen them show much emotion before and had never really thought of them as having deep feelings. Now he realized that they loved Cris deeply, just as he loved the members of his own family. They were human, and he had never really thought of them thus. Bewildered and unhappy with himself, he turned and went away.

After he left, Cris came slowly from the cottage. "I heard," he said, "and I'm sorry to have caused so much trouble. We'll find it hard to be separated, but I'll come to see you as often as I can." He hesitated, then added bitterly, "I've been sold just like a piece of furniture. Aunt Maria always said that it would be like this, and she was right.

"The Colonel could have made me free, if he had wanted to," he continued, turning to Prince. "You're supposed to be his favorite, and he should have done it for you, but he didn't. Instead he sold me so that he could make money on me." Seeing the sadness in his parents' faces, he added, "I'll keep in touch with you, but I'll be free someday. I swear I will."

Finally Prince spoke. "This has greatly upset

118

me, son. I never expected the Colonel would sell any of us, but we're his property. Remember that I have taught you to be a hard worker, useful and honest at all times."

"I'll remember, Father." Cris put his arms around his mother, who suddenly seemed very small as she huddled on her stool and wiped away her tears.

"Remember that we are descendants of praying Indians, son," she said. "We believe in God. Obey any and all laws, and if you feel hatred for your master, repeat this little prayer to yourself—Amanaomen Jehovah Jahassen metagh—take away, Lord, my stony heart—and the Lord will take care of you."

Cris kissed his mother and went inside to get his things together. Tomorrow he would leave for a new home to serve a new master. His heart was sad, but deep within him there burned a determination that he would someday be free.

Cris Runs Away

DEACON BROWN carried on two important kinds of business. He bought and sold cattle, and he ran a chandler's shop for making candles.

In time Cris became a good judge of cattle, and was allowed to buy and sell cattle on his own. When he wasn't buying and selling cattle, he worked in the chandler's shop. In general, he hardly realized that he was a slave, except that he couldn't come and go without reporting.

At first he greatly missed his family and friends back at his old home. He lived so far away that he couldn't go to see them often. Now he had to make new friends.

In making new friends, he met people doing several new and different kinds of work. Among others he had an opportunity to become acquainted with shipbuilders and sailors, some of whom came from Boston. The better he came to know these persons, the more interested he became in working on ships and going to sea.

As time passed, Deacon Brown came to trust Cris more and more and allowed him great freedom. He allowed him to travel widely to look after business. Sometimes he allowed him to go to Boston and to visit places along the Massachusetts coast by boat.

Cris greatly enjoyed these trips, especially taking voyages from Boston to other ports along the Massachusetts coast. At the same time, he heard many things about seafaring that he had never known before. The more that he learned about it, the more interested he became. Everything about it seemed exciting.

In time Cris began to learn the names of some of the ships. He learned which ships came to Boston regularly and which came only now and then. Somehow seeing these ships seemed to make him want more than ever to become free. Someday he would slip aboard one of the ships and sail away, never to return.

By now Cris was a huge man, powerful and brave, almost to recklessness. He was handsome, jolly, and made friends wherever he went. Now and then he made trips to Framingham to visit his parents and some of his old friends. His parents were proud of him and thought that he was satisfied with his new life.

After ten years of faithful service to Deacon Brown, Cris felt that he had earned the right to be free. He was ready to become a sailor and had even decided what kind of a ship he wanted to sail on.

One of the leading industries of the New England colonies was whaling or fishing for whales. Adventurous sea captains and their crews sailed the seven seas in specially built vessels, searching for whales. When the whales were caught, they were cut up and their blubber or fat was boiled to obtain an oil, known as sperm oil. One whale would yield at least eighty barrels of sperm oil.

The sperm oil was used largely for making candles. In those days many candles were used because most people used candles for lighting their homes. Deacon Brown used large quantities of sperm oil in his chandler shop.

In his work for Deacon Brown, Cris learned much about the whaling industry. He liked the idea of whaling and became eager to work on a whaling vessel. He realized, however, that he couldn't work on a vessel that would come back to Boston. If he left, he could never return.

Cris studied carefully all the whaling ships

that came to Boston. He wanted to know which ones called Boston home, and which ones called other ports home. He was interested in ships that had never come to Boston before.

Finally he found the right ship and decided definitely to run away. This ship was new to Boston and probably would never return.

The day before the ship was to leave, Cris hid near the wharf. When evening came, he decided to board the ship and talk with Captain Folger, who owned the ship. He would ask Captain Folger if he could join his crew.

"Good evening, sir," Cris said boldly, not as a slave but as any other man might speak. "I would like to join your crew."

Captain Folger studied the young man very carefully. Cris was just the sort of crewman he needed, but even in the darkness he could see that Cris had a strange complexion. At first he said nothing, but he wondered whether Cris was a free man or whether he was a slave. He didn't want to get into trouble by choosing someone's slave for his crew. At last he asked, "Do you live around here?"

"Of course, sir," Cris said quickly. He held his breath, waiting to see whether the captain believed him. He could feel hot blood running in his veins and pounding in his head. Did the captain suspect that he was a slave trying to run away?

The captain came closer and looked directly into Cris's eyes, as if to find out whether or not Cris was telling the truth. Cris stood erect, almost afraid to breathe.

"I've never been here before and never intend to return," said the captain. "I'm a stranger here, so I need to ask questions. I want to leave in the morning and I can't afford to have trouble!" He still looked carefully at Cris, as if trying to decide something about him.

Actually the captain was afraid that Cris was a slave, but he didn't want to ask Cris. All the slaves he had seen were black, but Cris was olive. "I can't afford to have trouble," the captain muttered almost to himself.

"You won't have any trouble, sir," Cris said. "I was born down by the turnpike not far from here, and my parents still live there. They know that I want to become a sailor and want me to succeed. If you employ me, I'll work hard as a member of your crew."

Just at this moment Deacon Brown and two other men came walking toward the ship. Cris saw them and was too frightened to continue speaking, even if he had wanted to. He wished that he could break away and run, but he was almost too frightened to move. Would the deacon come aboard and find him?

Deacon Brown and the two men came closer to the ship, but Cris pretended not to look at them.

The captain saw them and said, "I see I have visitors coming. Well, I'll take you," and motioned for Cris to go on below. Then he noticed that Cris looked extremely pale. "What's the trouble? Do you feel sick?"

"Yes, sir. I feel a little sick," said Cris, "but I'll feel better soon. You see, I haven't eaten all day, waiting for a chance to talk with you." Cris had thought that he had more courage and was surprised to feel afraid. Now he didn't know whether he wanted his freedom or not.

"Go down below," said Captain Folger, "and ask the cook to feed you. I can't afford to lose a good whaler." He gave Cris a gentle shove toward the steps to the lower deck. Cris was so weak that he almost fell down the steps.

As Cris disappeared, he could see the deacon and his friends coming aboard. "Why was the deacon coming here," he wondered. "This was a strange ship and the deacon didn't know Captain Folger." Cris decided to wait on the steps and listen to find out what the deacon wanted.

"May I help you, gentlemen?" he heard the captain say.

"Yes, you may," the deacon replied. "How long will you be in port?"

"Not very long," the captain replied. "I plan to leave at dawn tomorrow. Is there anything I can do for you?"

Deacon Brown hesitated, then said, "I am trying to buy sperm oil. I own a chandler shop not far from here and was hoping I could purchase some oil from you."

"I wish that I could help you," said the captain, "but I have sold all my oil."

"Possibly you'll have some next time," said the deacon. "Will you be back soon?"

Cris knew that this ship was not supposed to return to Boston, but he held his breath until the captain replied.

"No, I won't be back soon. I'm off course and don't belong here, but my friend Captain Drover should be here in a few days. He will have a great deal of oil. Will that help you?"

"No, I need oil immediately," replied the deacon. "If you haven't any, I'll send my man Cris to Nantucket tomorrow to get some. Thank you."

Cris heard the deacon moving toward the gangplank, with the two men behind him. Captain Folger followed them to see them off safely.

"Good night," said the deacon.

"Good night to you," said Captain Folger.

Cris heaved a sigh of relief and went on to find the cook. His knees were still weak, and he felt ashamed for having been so frightened. If he was to be a free man, he would need to have courage and keep a cool head.

On October 2, 1750, several days after Captain Folger had put out to sea, a notice appeared in the Boston *Gazette*. It read as follows:

"Ran away from his master William Brown of Framingham on the 30th of Sept. last a mulatto fellow about 27 years of age, named Crispus, 6 feet and 2 inches high, short curl'd hair, his knees nearer together than common; and had on a light colour'd beaver skin coat, plain new buckskin breeches, blue yarn stockings and a checked woolen shirt. Whoever shall take up said runaway and convey him to his aforesaid master shall have 10 pounds old tenor reward, and all necessary charges paid. And all masters of vessels and others are hereby cautioned against concealing or carrying off said servant on penalty of law."

At first Deacon Brown could scarcely believe that Cris had run away. He had sent Cris to Boston many times on business, but Cris always had returned on schedule. He had thought that Cris was happy with his work and that he had never thought of running away.

The deacon went to the Colonel's farm to talk

with Prince and his wife, but neither of them could tell him anything. They knew that earlier Cris had wanted to work on ships, but knew nothing of his later plans to run away. They were as much surprised as the deacon.

Secretly, Prince was glad that Cris was gone. He felt that Cris now would have a chance to lead the kind of life that he had always wanted to lead. His wife felt differently. She was worried about Cris and prayed for his safety.

Cris Becomes a Sailor

EARLY THE NEXT morning Captain Folger sent for Cris to come on deck. He was standing by the steersman at the wheel of the ship.

"Good morning, sir," Cris said as he reached the deck where the captain was waiting.

The captain studied Cris closely with his piercing eyes. "Good morning, Attucks," he said at last. "How do you feel today?"

"Fine, sir. The food and rest did me good. I'm ready to go to work."

"As you've probably noticed, we're already at sea," the captain went on. "Now that we're on our way, I'll tell you why I accepted you. I need a harpooner. Do you know what a harpooner does on a whaling vessel?"

"Not exactly, sir," Cris admitted. "Few whaling vessels come to Boston."

"Well, a harpooner is one of the most important men on a whaler. He handles the harpoon. Do you know what a harpoon is?"

"I've seen one, sir. It's a long shaft with a barbed iron point, fastened to a rope."

"Right, Attucks. A harpooner must throw a harpoon at a whale with such force that the iron point sinks into the whale's body and will not come out. He must be intelligent and alert and both strong and bold. At the same time he must be able to stay calm regardless of circumstances. As you can see, his work is extremely hard and dangerous."

Captain Folger paused and looked at Cris to see whether Cris showed any fear, but he saw no sign of weakness. He went on talking.

"There are seven kinds of whales in the sea, but we hunt only two. We look for whales that provide whalebone and whales that provide fat for making sperm oil. These two products are very important."

"Yes, I know. I used to work for a man who used sperm oil for making candles."

"As I have said, whaling is a hard and dangerous business," the captain continued, "but it is a very profitable business. We can always find a market for whalebone and sperm oil, no matter how much or little we have. Also we get meat from whales, and eat it almost constantly aboard ship. It's almost the only fresh meat we have, for we often stay at sea for a year and a half to two years at a time."

The captain paused to study Cris closely again, then continued. "Now, to get back to your job. You will need to take the place of a seaman who was injured on our last voyage. A harpooner must try to strike a whale hard enough and at the right spot to kill it. Sometimes he misses and must throw several harpoons at the whale before he hits a vital spot. Again I repeat that the job is hard and requires great courage. Do you want to try it, Attucks?"

"Yes, sir," Cris said without hesitation.

"There is always danger, you understand, that you'll be thrown overboard or crippled for life, or even lost at sea. A whale is a large and powerful animal, and very fast. When it is struck by a harpoon, it tries to escape and swims away at great speed."

"Yes, I can imagine," said Cris.

"One thing I haven't told you," the captain went on. "You'll have to throw the harpoon from small whaleboats like those you see here beside you. You can't throw the harpoon from the deck of this big vessel."

Cris looked at the small whaleboats on the

deck. Each boat was about thirty feet long, six feet wide, and pointed at both ends. "The harpooner stands in the bow," the captain explained. "Behind him are four men pulling the oars, and a fifth man steering the boat.

"Now let us imagine, Attucks, that you are standing in one of those boats, and that you have harpooned and wounded a whale. The whale swims away at top speed, maybe twenty-five miles an hour, pulling the boat behind it. The rope from the harpoon unwinds from a coil in a barrel at your feet. You must be careful not to get a leg or a foot caught in that rope, as Jansen did on our last voyage. Jansen is the seaman you're going to replace."

The captain paused to catch his breath and seemed satisfied that Cris could do the work. "Possibly you would like to think about the job before you decide to take it. You also can have a job as an ordinary seaman, which would pay you well, but you would make more money as a harpooner. We all share in the money that we get from selling oil and whalebone."

"I don't have to think, sir," said Cris with determination. "I want to be a harpooner."

"Good!" The captain smiled and gripped Cris firmly by the hand. "Go below and find Jansen. He will teach you how to throw the harpoon. Good luck, my boy."

Cris was an apt pupil and learned very fast. He worked with Jansen for several months as an apprentice, learning everything that Jansen could teach him. Jansen now wore a peg leg to take the place of the leg he had lost on the last voyage. This peg leg constantly reminded Cris that he must always be alert, cool, and bold.

At last a day came when Cris had an opportunity to test his training as a harpooner. The sun shone over the ocean and the weather was neither cool nor warm. The sturdy whaling vessel coasted along over the calm sea, with all sails set but hanging limply in the light breeze.

The ship was now sailing in waters where whales could be found. The captain stood beside the steersman at the wheel of the vessel. A man high in the crow's nest on the mainmast watched intently for a spout of mixed water and air to rise above the waves. That spout would show that a whale was near.

Cris and Jansen leaned against the ship's rail close by their whaleboat, watching the sea and talking. "Why do whales send up spouts of water?" asked Cris. "Spouting like that makes them easier to catch."

"Well, whales are mammals, and their bodies have lungs and warm blood, like yours and mine. They can stay under water for an hour or more, but every so often they have to come up to breathe. They have to come to the surface of the water to fill their lungs with fresh air.

"When a whale reaches the surface, it exhales or blows old, warm, moist air from its lungs. The air comes out through a hole in the top of its head and looks like a spout of steam. When we see a spout, we know that a whale has come to the surface to breathe."

Suddenly the lookout shouted, "A whale! There's a whale!"

"It's over there!" Jansen pointed excitedly off the starboard or right side of the ship.

"Boats away!" ordered the captain.

Attucks, Jansen, and their crew jumped quickly into their boat and were lowered to the water. "Bend, men, bend!" Attucks shouted to the oarsmen. The oarsmen pulled at their oars and the boats sped toward the whale.

When the boat approached the whale, the men ceased rowing and Cris stood up in the bow. He picked up the harpoon with its long shaft and sharp iron point. He checked the rope to be sure it would run freely from the barrel. There were 180 feet of rope in the barrel, and he didn't want it to tangle or catch. Then he turned to study the whale carefully.

Jansen watched him. He saw that Cris was a little nervous. "Steady, boy," he said in a reassuring, low voice. "Keep a cool head and a bold front and aim to kill."

Cris didn't answer, but nodded to indicate that he had heard. He gripped the harpoon with both hands and raised it high over his head. Then he took careful and determined aim and hurled the harpoon with all his strength at the whale's back. It struck the whale's body and the barb sank deep in the whale's flesh.

At first the whale was quiet, but in a moment it burst into frenzied activity. Its huge tail smashed the water and sent a cloudy spray flying in every direction.

"Back, men, back!" Cris shouted.

Cris feared that the whale would attack the boat, but suddenly it stopped splashing and dived beneath the surface. As it went down, it pulled the rope from the barrel and over the side of the boat so fast that it began to smoke. There was danger the rope would burn.

"Wet the rope!" Cris yelled to the men. "Don't let it burn."

A man stopped rowing and began to splash water on the rope to keep it from burning. The whale dived deeper and deeper and pulled the rope tighter and tighter. Then it slowed down and the rope slackened.

"Keep the rope tight," Cris ordered. "Pull the boat back!"

The men started to row backward, but suddenly the whale surfaced again. Then it plowed straight ahead, pulling the boat at a furious rate of speed. The boat fairly flew through the water.

"Hold on, men!" Cris shouted.

Jansen watched carefully. This was the same kind of fight with a whale in which he had been crippled. He wondered whether Cris would show enough courage and take the right step to capture the whale.

Cris was calm. He watched the whale closely with another harpoon in his hands, waiting for an opportunity to strike again. Shortly, the whale slowed down a trifle, and he ordered the men to pull in the rope to bring the boat in closer. Then, holding the harpoon high, he took steady aim and threw. This time the harpoon hit a vital spot on the whale.

The great animal thrashed wildly, but soon began to quiet down. The water about its body became stained with blood. The men in the boat began to cheer. They had been through enough encounters before to know that the whale had been mortally wounded.

"Good work, Attucks!" Jansen cried. He

reached forward and clapped Cris on the shoulder to show that he was greatly pleased.

Cris nodded as the others congratulated him, but still kept his eyes on the whale. He knew that a dying whale could be very dangerous. Suddenly the whale's tail lashed out again, and hit the surface of the water.

"Pull away," Cris shouted. "Pull the boat away from that tail."

The men rowed furiously to move the boat a safe distance away. The huge tail flailing the water could have flattened the boat in an instant. The whale's struggle with death was an awesome sight to behold. At last the struggle weakened and came to a stop. The huge animal was dead. Cris was glad when the ordeal was over. He sighed with relief and pride.

The men cheered and Jansen clapped Cris again on the shoulders. "A fine job," he said. "I knew that you could do it."

The men rowed over to recover the harpoons from the whale. Jansen stuck a flag in the whale's back and signaled the large whaling vessel to come and get the whale.

Cris sat down, exhausted. When the mother ship drew close, he climbed aboard wearily.

"How did you like it, Attucks?" asked Captain Folger with a smile. "Do you still want to be a harpooner on my ship?"

"Yes, sir," was all Cris could say. He was too exhausted to talk.

"I'm proud of you," the captain added. "You have what it takes. Now go below and have a good meal." He slapped Cris on the back.

Cris went below, but he ate little. Instead, he crawled into his bunk and immediately fell asleep. He slept like a log for several hours.

When he awoke, refreshed, he thought back over the day. He had caught his first whale, and felt both excited and proud. At the same time, he felt a challenge to look to the future. He, Crispus Attucks, runaway slave, would prove himself to be a real man. He would work hard as a harpooner and become the most valuable member of Captain Folger's crew.

Cris still could scarcely believe that he was free—no longer a slave. If he was free, he must have a great ambition for the future. He must become a trusted and daring harpooner.

Cris Visits His Parents

THE YEARS passed swiftly and young Attucks became the most fearless and most valuable whaler on Captain Folger's ship. He loved his work, and the men respected him for his courage and good judgment. He was accepted by the crew as a free man, and nobody ever hinted that he might have been a slave.

From time to time, every few years, Captain Folger's ship stopped at ports not far from Framingham. When this happened, Cris slipped away at night to visit his parents. He had to go secretly to their cottage to avoid being seen, for legally he was still a slave.

Deacon Brown had long since stopped looking for Cris, but by law he was still a runaway slave. If he were discovered or identified, he could be returned to his former master. He still was not legally free.

By this time he had become a great mystery around Framingham. He had been a trusted slave, free to come and go largely as he pleased. Now no one knew how he had escaped, or why he had gone. Everyone wondered about him.

Some years after young Attucks disappeared, Colonel Buckminster became seriously ill. By now he was a broken old man and he grew steadily worse. Finally he felt that his last days were at hand and asked to see Prince.

"Send for Prince," he told his wife. "I want to talk with him."

"Don't tax your strength," Mrs. Buckminster cautioned. "You can talk with him later."

"I must talk with him now," he insisted.

Prince hurried to the Big House to see the sick Colonel. He no longer was angry at the Colonel for having sold Cris. Secretly he was glad, for Cris now had the freedom that he had always wanted, even as a little boy.

"Good morning, Prince," said Mrs. Buckminster warmly when he came to the Colonel's house.

"Good morning, Ma'am," Prince said. "How is the Colonel?"

"Not good, Prince. He wants to see you." She led the way through the house to the Colonel's bedroom. The Colonel lay sunken far down under the covers with only his snow-white hair and pale face to be seen. His eyes, surrounded by dark circles, were closed, and his face was wrinkled with age and weariness.

Quietly Prince took a chair beside the bed and waited for the Colonel to open his eyes and to speak. When the Colonel saw Prince, he smiled weakly and put out his hand.

Prince took the Colonel's hand and held it gently. "How are you, sir?" he asked.

"I'm not long for this world, Prince," the Colonel said weakly.

"You must not give up, sir."

The Colonel smiled again. "We must not fool ourselves, Prince. We all get old and wither away. Then our time comes." He paused and tried to pull himself up in the bed.

"May I help you, sir?" Prince put an extra pillow under the Colonel's head.

"Thank you. I have long wanted to talk with you, Prince. You have always been faithful to me, even after I sold your son."

Prince dropped his head and wondered what the Colonel was about to say. He still respected his owner as a good man.

"After I die, my son, Thomas, will take over everything I have," the Colonel went on. "He will take possession of the slaves as part of my property. You have never seemed like a slave to me, and I would like to make you free. I'll have the papers made out for you." The Colonel paused to rest for a moment. "What do you say, Prince?" He waited for an answer.

"Thank you, Colonel," said Prince. "I never expected you to offer me freedom, but I cannot accept. I, too, am growing old, and freedom at my age would not help me. I have given you the best years of my life, and granting me freedom now would be like casting me out."

A single tear stole down the Colonel's cheek. Finally he opened his eyes to meet those of his faithful slave. "Yes, you have given me the best years of your life, Prince, and you have never complained. I can see how you feel."

The Colonel paused wearily, then continued. "I'll name your home near the turnpike Prince's Meadow. You may live there as long as you please and you'll be free to come and go as a free man. You'll remain the property of my son Thomas, but you won't need to work."

"Thank you, Colonel," said Prince. "You have been very kind to me, and I have been happy under the circumstances." He gripped the Colonel's hand and was gone.

By this time it was dusk. Prince hurried home, eager to tell his wife about his visit with the Colonel. When he neared the cottage, he noticed that the curtains were drawn. Then he was almost certain that Cris was there.

Prince's guess was right. When he stepped inside the house, he saw a tall muscular young man putting logs on the fire. Phebe, who had never married, sat fingering a few trinkets that Cris had brought her. Mrs. Attucks was putting food on the table for supper.

"Father!" Cris gripped his father's hand and looked down at him.

Prince looked up at his son with pride. "I

certainly am glad to see you, son," he said. "Have you been here long?"

"Only a few minutes, Father," replied Cris. "Let me show you some of the gifts I have brought home." He opened a large bag and brought out one gift after another. Prince made Cris tell something about each gift.

"I'm really glad you're free, son," he said calmly after Cris stopped bringing out gifts. "The Colonel offered me my freedom when I visited him tonight, but I refused."

"Why, Father?"

"Where could I go now? What could I do? When I was young, I could have made my way, but I have given my life to the Colonel. Now that I am old, I need someone to take care of me."

At first Cris did not speak. Then he said, "You're right, Father. When I was young, I talked about freedom all the time, but I never guessed you wanted to be free yourself."

"I suppose I did," admitted Prince.

"Come and eat," called Mrs. Attucks quietly, as if hating to disturb the conversation. "You men eat alone and talk."

Father and son sat down at the table to continue their conversation. Mrs. Attucks and Phebe sat in a corner of the room and looked at the interesting gifts. After supper, the family talked far into the night.

The time always passed fast when Cris came home. Everyone felt that each trip might be his last, so there was much happiness and joy with everyone sharing in the conversation.

On his trips home, Cris never went behind the Big House to visit the slave quarters. He even stayed away from Aunt Maria, who had finally learned to live without Cato. On one of his visits, however, Prince told him she was ill.

"I should go to see her," he said to his parents. "She is old and sick, and I would not feel right if I didn't at least look in on her. She was always good to me."

At first Prince and his wife said nothing. Then Prince said, "I learned long ago that I couldn't stop you from doing what you wanted to do. I used to object to your going to see Aunt Maria, but in recent years she has become a great influence for good among young people. Go to her cabin to see her son, but take Phebe with you. Legally you're still a runaway slave, and I wouldn't want you to get caught."

"You're right, Father," Cris agreed. "Perhaps Phebe should go with me."

"Watch out for Little John, Phebe," Prince said. "He never liked Cris and probably would turn him in, if he got a chance."

"I'll find him and keep him entertained while Cris visits Aunt Maria," said Phebe.

She and Cris slipped out a back way to Aunt Maria's cottage. They walked along cautiously.

Phebe had never married. Several of the slaves had been interested in her, but she had seemed content to work in the Big House and come home to her parents at night. Finally most of the men of her age were already married.

One slave, who was still unmarried, was Little John, but he couldn't be trusted. Somehow he took special delight in telling untrue things about other slaves. Consequently, the other slaves had little use for him. The only people who liked him were little children. They enjoyed him because he was a good storyteller.

Phebe found Little John in a cabin with some children. The children were sitting around him, listening to one of his tales.

Phebe walked into the cabin and joined the group. "What brings you here?" Little John asked her, suspiciously.

"I just got tired of being at home and decided to take a walk," Phebe replied.

Little John looked as if he wondered whether or not he had missed something he ought to know. "It's too dark for you to take such a long walk alone," he said. "Are you sure you came alone?" He started to get up to check.

"Forget about me and look after the children," said Phebe. "I'm old enough to look after myself in the dark. Go ahead with your story." She settled herself on a vacant stool. The children smiled at her.

Little John settled back and continued his story. Phebe appeared deeply interested.

In the meantime Cris had proceeded directly to Aunt Maria's cabin. When she saw Cris, her wrinkled face broke into a smile. "Sit down," she said. "I'm glad to see you." Cris took her weak hand and pressed it warmly.

"I've only a few minutes," he said, "but I wanted to wish you well."

"Save your breath, Cris. I won't get well. It

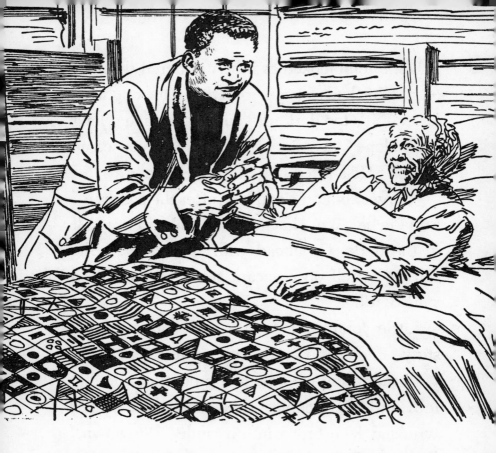

is just a matter of days. I know a lot about sickness. This is my end."

"Don't give up, Aunt Maria," said Cris. "Take some of your herbs and pills."

Aunt Maria smiled again. "I wish things were

160

that simple. There's no cure for my sickness, son. I'm old, tired, and heartbroken. Soon I will steal away to Jesus."

"You never heard from Cato?" Cris asked.

"No, never," she replied. "He must have died. You had better not stay long, Cris. Deacon Tom will probably come here to see me this evening. I wouldn't want you to lose your freedom because you have come to visit me."

Just then there was a knock at the door. Cris and Aunt Maria looked at each other fearfully, but Cris was used to thinking quickly. He snatched a quilt from the foot of the bed and slid under the bed. Then he pulled in his arms and legs and hid under the quilt.

"Come in," Aunt Maria said weakly.

The door opened and Little John came in with Deacon Tom. Both men were out of breath and both seemed to be greatly excited.

"What's the hurry?" asked Aunt Maria softly.

"Are you all alone, Aunt Maria?" asked Deacon Tom, looking around the cabin.

"Yes," she answered. "Are you looking for someone, sir?"

"Not if you're alone," replied Deacon Tom. He looked angrily at Little John, who seemed to be disappointed. They left the cabin.

"Stay there until I call you, Cris," Aunt Maria whispered as the two unwanted visitors left. "I'm going outside to watch them."

The weak old slave crept out of bed, put a shawl around her shoulders, and eased outside. She carefully shut the door behind her to keep the light from shining upon her. She waited until she could no longer hear Little John and Deacon Tom talking in the darkness. Then she opened the door and whispered, "Come quickly."

Cris slid out from under the bed and went outside, closing the door quietly behind him. "Thank you, Aunt Maria," he said, "but you shouldn't have come out here." He kissed her wrinkled old forehead. "Now get back to bed."

"Hurry, Cris," she urged. "Go toward the creek. They'll never see you there."

"God bless you, Aunt Maria," he said as he hurried away. Phebe was watching and joined Cris a little way from Aunt Maria's cabin. She knew that Little John had told Deacon Tom something to make him suspicious.

No one ever talked with Aunt Maria again. After Cris left, she fell in front of the doorstep of her cabin. The next morning, someone found her there lying on the ground. Many people wondered why she was out of bed and where she had been, but no one ever knew.

This was the only trip that Cris made to the slave quarters when he came to visit his family. He always asked about the slaves, however, because he was interested in their welfare. At the same time, he realized that he didn't dare to be seen in the neighborhood. He already had had a narrow escape, and he didn't want to run the risk of another.

Crispus Attucks worked for many years on Captain Folger's whaling vessel. During those years, he never forgot his parents and his sister. He always visited them secretly at night when his ship stopped at a port near Framingham.

However, as the years passed, Captain Folger traveled more widely with his whaling vessel, and Cris found it more difficult to reach Framingham. Whaling voyages often lasted long periods of time. As a result, Cris sometimes didn't get to see his family for months or even a year or two at a time.

The last time Cris came home was September 5, 1769. His ship was in Boston at the time, awaiting a trip south, and he found an opportunity to slip back to Framingham.

On that day he had an unusually happy visit

with his family. When he bade his father, mother, and sister good-by and returned to Boston, neither he nor they realized that he would never come back. However, times were troubled in Massachusetts, and in the other colonies, too. Things were about to take place in which Crispus Attucks would have an opportunity to demonstrate his superior human qualities.

The Boston Massacre

CRISPUS ATTUCKS returned to Boston in the fall of 1769. At that time he found hard feelings among the people because King George III of England was attempting to rule the American colonies without regard for their rights. The colonists, especially in Massachusetts, complained that the mother country was unfair.

At last the King sent British soldiers to Boston to enforce the laws. The dispute between colonial leaders and the British government soon caused bad feeling between the soldiers and the townspeople.

One day James Otis, one of the colonial leaders, became involved in an argument with some British army officers. In the heat of the argument, one of the officers struck Otis over the head with a sword. Some time later Otis had mental trouble, and people said that the blow on his head was the cause. Otis's accident increased the feeling of anger which the people of Boston felt for the British soldiers.

Shortly after this happened, Attucks left Boston on a whaling voyage with Captain Folger. When he returned in February, 1770, trouble between the people of Boston and the soldiers had become even worse.

One day a crowd of citizens attacked a man named Richardson, whom they accused of being a traitor. When Richardson reached the safety of his own house, he fired on the crowd and killed a young boy and wounded another.

Attucks watched this event silently. Later he attended the boy's funeral and heard the boy

spoken of as a martyr to the cause of American freedom. Attucks was greatly impressed with those words, and became interested in the cause of freedom. He hoped his ship would not leave Boston until he could learn more about it.

When Richardson was tried for murder of the boy, Attucks was in the courtroom, watching and listening. He was greatly upset when Richardson was judged innocent and set free. He felt that Richardson should have been punished.

Twenty years before, Attucks had run away seeking freedom for himself. Now, as he listened to the Richardson trial, he became greatly interested in this new cause for freedom. He decided to seek freedom not only for himself but for the whole colony.

Attucks frequently mingled with crowds of men that gathered in the streets and squares. "What do you think about the way the King's soldiers are treating you?" he asked.

"We hate it," the men replied.

As days passed the soldiers and colonists hurled bitter remarks at one another and the tension mounted. It was not long before Attucks, to whom freedom grew dearer each day, became a leader of the colonists.

One Friday a street fight broke out between a group of townspeople and some soldiers, and several persons on both sides were hurt.

"This is disgraceful," declared John Adams, one of the colonial leaders, to the officer in command of the soldiers. "You must make an effort to control your men."

"And you must control the colonists," the officer replied. "They act like barbarians."

Over the weekend the situation grew worse. People gathered in groups to discuss what had happened. "This is the end," some said. "Blood will surely flow now."

The confusion grew worse when the soldiers

rushed from their barracks and threatened the people. They were armed with swords, muskets, bayonets, clubs, and anything else they could lay their hands on. They probably meant only to frighten people, but the colonists began to arm themselves with clubs.

Attucks spoke briefly to the crowd in the square. He mounted a platform that had been erected for speakers. The crowd pressed forward to listen as his voice boomed out.

"The way to be free is to strike out against those who would enslave you! You must stick together! You are in the right and must not be afraid. You must have courage."

He spoke to the crowd as if he had been speaking in public for years. Somehow, now he felt that he must bind these patriots together in a common cause, just as he had spoken to members of his crew on the ship to bind them together.

"We will not be taxed by the government of

Britain three thousand miles away!" one patriot cried. "We don't send representatives to the English Parliament. We tried to settle this tax business three years ago."

The crowd murmured its approval.

"So we did," another patriot said. "Samuel Adams stated our rights as Americans some time ago, but the King ignored his letter."

"What can we do?" asked a third man. "We came to this country to be free, but the King will not grant us even the freedom that other Englishmen enjoy."

"That's right," added a fourth patriot. "When the King demands our money, he gets all that we have. Conditions here today are no better than they once were in England."

The crowd nodded and looked at Attucks, who stood on the platform, listening. "The laws which Parliament has passed interfere with trade and enable English merchants to make greater profits at our expense," he said. "Then what did the King do when you refused to pay his taxes?" He pointed at the British soldiers near by. "It is not fair for the King to send soldiers here to enforce his unjust laws."

By now the soldiers were close behind the crowd. "Who says so?" shouted one soldier. Everyone turned to stare at him, and he clutched his musket as if intending to shoot.

"I say so," Attucks said boldly. "It is only cowards who mistreat others with guns in hand. If you would put down your guns we'd show you how to fight fairly."

Cries of "Yes! Yes!" rose from the crowd, and the soldier and his comrades retreated toward their barracks.

At that moment their commanding officer, a Captain Thomas Preston, came rushing forward. "Stop!" he shouted, purple with rage. "Stop this confusion!" He pointed up at Attucks. "Come down from there! Come down and stop arousing these people!"

Attucks turned to the crowd. "Go home and get some rest," he said. "Tomorrow things may clear up." Immediately the crowd began to move away in little groups and pairs, talking among themselves. When the square was empty, Attucks turned back to the Captain.

"So you think I'm arousing the people!" he said. "What do you think you and your men are doing? You're the ones who are stirring things up. The sight of you is as maddening as a red flag is to a bull." He strode off, leaving the Captain staring after him.

A little after nine o'clock on Monday night, March 5, 1770, fire bells began to ring. People rushed outdoors to look for a burning building. "Where's the fire?" they shouted.

They saw Attucks marching toward the square at the head of a small group of men.

"There is no fire," he told them. "The bells are calling all patriots out to help those who are already out."

"What's the trouble?" someone asked.

"Too many people are being hurt," Attucks said. "This is a bad situation. Surely the King knows things are growing worse."

By this time about twenty-eight people had gathered in the square. Some soldiers had gathered there, too.

One patriot pointed at the soldiers. "Look at them," he said. "They're bold now and threaten us with swords, guns, bayonets, and anything else they can lay their hands on."

"Yes, they won't leave us alone," another man said. "No one is safe."

"Women are afraid to leave their homes," added another. "Children are afraid to play outside. What are we to do?"

"Maybe the soldiers only mean to frighten us,

but they are making us angry instead," added still another.

Attucks listened to these remarks and noticed the fear on the faces of the speakers. At last he said, "I'm going down to the docks. I will return shortly." He hurried away.

Not long afterward, a soldier got into an argument with a young boy. The fire bell began to ring again. "Why is the bell ringing now? Where is the fire?" the soldier asked.

"There isn't any fire," said a patriot. "The bell is ringing to call out more people. We saw you pick a fight with Squire Holt's boy and we know no one is safe. We're calling people out for our own protection." He joined the crowd that was assembling in the square.

Bells were ringing everywhere now, sounding the alarm. The patriots shouted threateningly at the soldiers, and the soldiers shouted back in the same manner. A group of patriots gathered around the boy and shook their makeshift weapons defiantly. The soldiers fell back and sent for Captain Preston, who hurried to the square with eight additional men.

The warlike, determined attitude of the Captain and his men alarmed the patriots. They looked around for Attucks, and when they failed to see him some of them ran.

Finally someone shouted, "Here he comes!" and everyone turned to look. Attucks came striding up Cornhill Street followed by fifty or sixty men, mostly sailors—a giant of a man, reckless and bold, armed with a piece of cordwood.

A light snow had fallen during the day, but now the moon was shining on the cold, snow-covered street. Suddenly the night was quiet except for the shuffle of the sailors' feet.

A few soldiers fled, but Captain Preston and his eight men stood firm, watching Attucks and the sailors approach, chanting.

"The way to get rid of these soldiers is to attack the main guard," Attucks told his men. "Strike at the root!" He reached the soldiers and stopped at the very tips of their bayonets. "This is the nest," he said.

The crowd grew quiet and tense. "You are cowards for bringing guns against unarmed people," Attucks told the Captain. "Put down your guns and let us settle this man to man."

Someone in the crowd threw a rock at the soldiers. Then others struck at the soldiers' guns with their sticks. Suddenly Crispus Attucks' challenge was answered by a shout—"Fire!"

No one knew who gave the order, but at the first shot, fired by a soldier named Montgomery, Crispus Attucks fell dead. Four of his companions also fell. Two, Samuel Gray and James Caldwell, were killed immediately on the spot, and the other two, Samuel Maverick and Patrick Carr, died a day or two later.

When the shooting occurred, Samuel Adams was a block away in Fanueil Hall. Hearing the shots, he ran excitedly into the streets and shouted, "Stop this disgraceful exhibition!" Soon he came upon the still forms of Attucks and the others and stopped short, crying, "Lord have mercy on us all!"

Thursday, March 8, 1770, was a solemn day in Boston, one of the most solemn in the city's history. All the bells in the city, and those in neighboring Charlestown and Roxbury, tolled to announce the funeral of four victims of the Boston Massacre.

The bodies of Attucks and Caldwell, who were strangers in town, had been taken to Fanueil Hall. The bodies of Maverick and Gray had been taken to the homes of their families. The four hearses bearing the bodies met near the Custom House, the scene of the fighting. From there they proceeded to the Middle Burying Ground, one of the city's oldest cemeteries.

An immense crowd of people followed the hearses through the streets to pay tribute to the fallen men. First came the poorer people of the city, marching six abreast on foot. Behind them came carriages belonging to the city's leading citizens. Everyone wanted to show the King and his government how Boston felt about the death of the patriots.

Samuel Adams and other patriots had helped to plan the solemn procession which followed the hearses through the streets. They knew that the people were greatly shocked and wanted to keep them aroused. They knew that the time was near to fight for independence and wanted everyone to be ready to fight.

When the procession reached the Middle Burying Ground, the people gathered around and watched the four victims lowered to a single grave with solemn ceremony. The weather was still wintry, but neither the sunless sky nor the frosty air tempted them to hurry home. They lingered about the grave or gathered in small groups to discuss the tragic and exciting event which had happened. Everyone feared that greater trouble would come in the days ahead.

The people were both stunned and aroused. An article in a Boston newspaper described the deaths of the patriots as follows: "The aggravated circumstances of their death, the distress and sorrow visible in every countenance, together with the peculiar solemnity with which the funeral was conducted surpasses description."

Later in the day a large crowd assembled in Dock Square to hear a memorial ceremony. Their heads were bowed and uncovered.

Various people rose to speak about the massacre, as the people of Boston called the fight.

One after another they paid tribute to the brave men who had fallen. Several speeches made special mention of Crispus Attucks.

"If a crisis makes a man, this Boston Massacre accounts for Crispus Attucks," said one of the speakers. "It filled him with a passion for freedom; caused him to be intolerant of intolerance; endowed him with native daring; made him courageous to lead even under adverse and unfavorable conditions. If a crisis does not make a man, he would have been great without the occurrence of the Boston Massacre."

The ceremony was brief, but impressive. At the close a minister read from the Bible, and spoke solemnly to the hushed crowd. "Let us pay solemn tribute to these men who died for us," he said looking out at his audience. "Remember that we came to these shores seeking freedom, yet tyranny exists here. These men acted for the welfare of us all.

"The first to fall in the massacre was Crispus Attucks, a hero forty-seven years of age. He was born a slave, who ran away from his master in Framingham, and has earned an honest living on a whaling ship. As a seaman, he obviously came to feel keenly the restrictions which England has imposed on us. His death is significant because it demonstrates his loyalty to a country in which he was not actually free. In spite of this fact, he gave his life to help us get rid of the shackles that bind us. His sacrifice serves as a rallying cry for freedom.

"Eighteen centuries before Attucks became a martyr for our welfare," the minister went on, "legend tells us that a Negro bore the cross to Calvary for Jesus. Now as we colonists struggle wearily under our cross of woe, a second Negro has come to the front to bear the cross and relieve our suffering.

"Let us bow our heads in a moment of silence."

184

All heads dropped and stayed down until the minister spoke again. "Someone has written a poem to commemorate this day," he said. "The verses were circulated about the city earlier. Let us read the lines together."

"Well-fated shades! Let no unmanly tear
   From Pity's eye disdain your honored bier;
   Lost to their view, surviving friends may
      mourn,
   Yet o'er thy pile shall flames celestial burn;
   Long as in Freedom's cause the wise contend,
   Dear to your country shall your fame extend,
   While to the world the lettered stone shall
      tell
   How Caldwell, Attucks, Gray, and Maverick
      fell."

A few days later one of the leading patriots, John Adams, wrote a letter to one of his friends. In this letter he described Attucks' role of leadership in these words: "This was the declaration of war and it has been fulfilled. The world has heard from Crispus Attucks, and more important, the English-speaking world will never forget his noble daring and his excusable rashness in the holy cause of liberty."

On a later occasion Adams wrote these words about Attucks and the four men who died with him before the Custom House: "On that night the formation of American Independence was laid. . . . The death of four or five persons, the most obscure and inconsiderable that could have been found upon the continent, has never yet been forgiven by any part of America."

News of the Boston Massacre spread to the other colonies. More than any other incident of the time, it helped to unite the colonies. It demonstrated that the rights of the colonists were being endangered more and more and that the colonists might have to fight soon for their freedom. It served greatly to strengthen animosity

186

toward the King of England and his government. Now that Massachusetts had shown resistance to taxation without representation, other colonies began to show resistance, too.

Much has been written about the beginnings of the American Revolution. Strangely enough, few United States history books have ever given sufficient attention or credit to Crispus Attucks, the first to fall for American Independence.

A Monument Is Erected

IN 1886 the spots where Crispus Attucks and Samuel Gray fell during the Boston Massacre were marked by circles on the pavement. Within each circle there was a hub with spokes leading out to form a wheel.

The following year, the state of Massachusetts appropriated money to erect a monument in memory of Attucks and his fallen comrades. Attucks' name was to head the list as the first to fall for independence.

Most people favored appropriating money to build the monument, but some objected. Those who objected argued that the Boston Massacre could have been avoided. They said that Attucks and the others should not have antagonized the British soldiers.

Those favoring the appropriation replied, "They were not trying to cause trouble. They simply were patriots seeking freedom."

The objectors argued further, "These men only represented the working class. They did not represent the true patriots of the revolution."

The supporters replied, "You are wrong in this conclusion. The members of the working class went to the front in large numbers to fight for freedom. They helped to make up the backbone of the Revolutionary Army."

Other supporters said, "The Boston Massacre brought us ten years closer to freedom. Let's not forget these brave men who forged the way for the freedom which we enjoy today."

Someone read the following words from Daniel Webster to the Assembly, which was considering the appropriation: "From that moment we may date the severance of the British Empire." Webster had written these words years before, but they had great influence on the assembly. The members voted to make the necessary appropriation for building the monument.

One year later the monument to honor Crispus Attucks and his brave companions was erected. It is a large structure, over twenty-five feet high and a little over ten feet wide.

The bas-relief or raised portion on the face of the main part of the monument portrays the Boston Massacre with Crispus Attucks lying in the foreground. In the upper lefthand corner is an inscription, which reads: "From that moment we may date the severance of the British Empire. . . . Daniel Webster." In the upper righthand corner is another inscription, reading: "On that night the foundation of American Independence was laid. . . . John Adams."

190

Under the scene is the date, March 5, 1770.

Above the bas-relief stands a female figure, "Free America," with a serious, determined, and heroic expression on her upturned face. With her left hand she clasps a flag about to be unfurled, and in her right hand she holds the broken chain of oppression. Beneath her right foot she crushes the royal crown of England, which lies torn and twisted on the ground.

At the left of the figure, clinging to the edge of the base, is an eagle. This eagle has its wings raised and its beak open, showing that it has just alighted. Its pose enhances the fiery spirit of the female figure.

Thirteen stars are cut into one of the faces of the monument. Beneath these stars in raised letters are the names of Crispus Attucks, Samuel Gray, James Caldwell, Samuel Maverick, and Patrick Carr.

The unveiling of the monument, including the

ceremony, was an impressive event. The chief speaker was the celebrated writer and lecturer, John Fiske. The poet J. Boyle O'Reilly wrote the following poem especially for the occasion.

"And honor to Crispus Attucks
Who was the leader and voice that day:
    The first to defy
    And the first to die,
    With Maverick, Carr, and Gray.
Call it riot or revolution,
Or mob or crowd as you may . . .
    Such deaths have been seed of nations,
    Such lives shall be honored for aye . . ."